Taxcafe.co.uk Tax Guides

Small Business Tax Saving Tactics 2016/17

By Carl Bayley BSc ACA
and
Nick Braun PhD

Important Legal Notices:

Taxcafe®
Tax Guide - "Small Business Tax Saving Tactics"

Published by:
Taxcafe UK Limited
67 Milton Road
Kirkcaldy KY1 1TL
Tel: (0044) 01592 560081
Email: team@taxcafe.co.uk

ISBN 978-1-911020-09-7

Fourth edition, August 2016

Disclaimer
Before reading or relying on the content of this tax guide please read the disclaimer.

Disclaimer

1. This guide is intended as **general guidance** only and does NOT constitute accountancy, tax, investment or other professional advice.

2. The authors and Taxcafe UK Limited make no representations or warranties with respect to the accuracy or completeness of this publication and cannot accept any responsibility or liability for any loss or risk, personal or otherwise, which may arise, directly or indirectly, from reliance on information contained in this publication.

3. Please note that tax legislation, the law and practices of Government and regulatory authorities (e.g. HM Revenue & Customs) are constantly changing. We therefore recommend that for accountancy, tax, investment or other professional advice, you consult a suitably qualified accountant, tax advisor, financial adviser, or other professional adviser.

4. Please also note that your personal circumstances may vary from the general examples provided in this guide and your professional adviser will be able to provide specific advice based on your personal circumstances.

5. This guide covers UK taxation only and any references to 'tax' or 'taxation', unless the contrary is expressly stated, refer to UK taxation only. Please note that references to the 'UK' do not include the Channel Islands or the Isle of Man. Foreign tax implications are beyond the scope of this guide.

6. All persons described in the examples in this guide are entirely fictional. Any similarities to actual persons, living or dead, or to fictional characters created by any other author, are entirely coincidental.

7. The views expressed in this publication are the authors' own personal views and do not necessarily reflect the views of any organisation which they may represent.

About the Authors & Taxcafe

Carl Bayley is the author of a series of Taxcafe guides designed specifically for the layman. Carl's particular speciality is his ability to take the weird, complex and inexplicable world of taxation and set it out in the kind of clear, straightforward language that taxpayers themselves can understand. As he often says himself, "my job is to translate 'tax' into English".

In addition to being a recognised author, Carl has often spoken on taxation on radio and television, including the BBC's It's Your Money programme and the Jeremy Vine Show on Radio 2.

A chartered accountant by training, Carl is currently Chairman of the Tax Faculty of the Institute of Chartered Accountants in England and Wales and is also a member of the Institute's governing Council.

Nick Braun founded Taxcafe.co.uk in 1999, along with his partner, Aileen Smith. As the driving force behind the company, their aim is to provide affordable plain-English tax information for private individuals and investors, business owners, IFAs and accountants.

Since then Taxcafe has become one of the best-known tax publishers in the UK and has won several business awards.

Nick has been involved in the tax publishing world since 1989 as a writer, editor and publisher. He holds a doctorate in economics from the University of Glasgow, where he was awarded the prestigious William Glen Scholarship and later became a Research Fellow. Prior to that, he graduated with distinction from the University of South Africa, the country's oldest university, earning the highest results in economics in the university's history.

Contents

Chapter 1

Introduction

The main purpose of this guide is to help self-employed business owners pay less Income Tax and National Insurance on their profits.

Most of the chapters will show you how to claim more tax deductible expenses or bigger tax deductible expenses.

Expenses are vital in business tax planning because, in simple terms, taxable profit is calculated as follows:

Taxable Profit = Income *less* Tax-Deductible Expenses

So the bigger your tax deductible expenses, the lower your taxable profit and the smaller your tax bill.

Lesser-known and Big Tax Deductions

Most business expenses are tax deductible, providing they are incurred 'wholly and exclusively' for business purposes.

You probably don't need us to tell you that stationery purchased for a business is a tax deductible expense, as is a salary paid to an employee.

The focus of this guide is not the obvious expenses. Our aim is to help you:

Claim tax deductions you didn't know about

and

Maximise big, important tax deductions

Lesser-known tax deductions may include the cost of travelling abroad on business or entertaining staff. They may also include paying wages to your minor children or claiming tax relief on your *home's* mortgage interest.

Maximising big important tax deductions may include paying your employees in more tax-efficient ways, increasing the tax relief on your motoring expenses, and maximising your property tax deductions.

Many of the tax planning ideas contained in this guide are not widely known or covered in other tax publications.

We are quite confident that even those with fairly substantial tax knowledge will uncover many useful nuggets that will help them save tax.

Capital Gains Tax & Inheritance Tax

The main focus of the guide is helping business owners pay less Income Tax and National Insurance. These are the taxes that have to be paid year in, year out and are levied at potentially extortionate rates.

Some of the later chapters of the guide also contain important information on reducing other taxes, including VAT, Capital Gains Tax and Inheritance Tax.

Tax Red Tape

The focus of this guide is tax planning, i.e. helping you pay less tax.

We do not spend any time explaining how to complete a tax return, compile accounts or do basic bookkeeping.

Whilst this is important, there are plenty of accountants out there who will help you with your tax compliance for a modest fee.

We feel business owners are far better served by a guide that focuses solely on helping them pay less tax.

Companies

This tax planning guide is aimed at self-employed business owners, namely:

- Sole traders, and
- Partnerships

It is not for company owners. Many of the tax rules that apply to sole traders and partnerships apply differently to company owners.

When putting this guide together we decided that it would make for easier reading if the target market was focused. Having lots of qualifiers and special rules for company owners would muddy the waters.

But don't worry, Taxcafe has a range of other guides aimed at company owners (go to *www.taxcafe.co.uk* for details).

Summary of Contents

The following is a brief chapter by chapter summary of the tax planning information contained in this guide:

Part 1 – Working from Home

Chapter 3 explains how you can maximise your tax deduction for home office expenses, including home mortgage interest, council tax, property repairs, and gas and electricity costs. This tax deduction can be claimed even if you only work from home some of the time.

Many part-time businesses are run from home and in Chapter 4 we take a look at the special tax rules that apply to this type of business, including the one that allows part-timers to offset business losses against their other taxable income, eg income from employment.

Part 2 – How Your Family Can Help You Save Tax

In Chapter 5 we look at how your spouse or partner can be employed in your business or made a partner and paid income that is either tax free or taxed less heavily than your own.

Chapter 6 explains how to save tax by employing your children (including your minor children) or making them partners in your business.

Part 3 – Employing People

When you take on employees you may have to pay employer's National Insurance. Chapter 7 explains how it's calculated and some of the new reliefs.

Chapter 8 looks at some of the tax-free benefits that can be paid to employees. These are useful alternatives to cash salary when economic conditions are tough.

Entertaining is not usually a tax deductible expense but certain staff entertainment costs are fully tax deductible. Chapter 9 explains how you can maximise your claim.

Larger employers already have to make compulsory pension contributions for their employees and this additional cost is gradually being extended to all employers. Chapter 10 explains how it operates.

Part 4 – Business Travel, Subsistence and Entertainment

Chapter 11 explains how you can claim a bigger tax deduction for your travel costs by making sure that more of your journeys are treated as business travel.

Chapter 12 explains how you can claim a bigger tax deduction for subsistence costs (including restaurant meals and alcohol) when you travel on business.

Entertainment costs are not tax deductible but, as we show in Chapter 13, it is possible to structure your spending so that these costs are partly tax deductible.

Chapter 14 looks at how you can claim a tax deduction for flights, hotels, meals and other costs when you travel abroad on business... even when you take some time out to relax!

Chapter 15 explains how you can claim the additional cost of travelling abroad with your spouse or partner.

Part 5 – Investing in Your Business: Capital Allowances

When you buy computers, motor vehicles and other equipment for your business you can claim capital allowances.

In Chapter 16 we explain how they are calculated and in Chapter 17 how you can claim extra tax relief by timing your capital spending carefully. You can even claim a cashback from the taxman, as we reveal in Chapter 18.

Part 6 – Leasing vs Buying Business Assets

What saves you more tax: leasing assets or buying them using HP? In Chapters 19 and 20 we explain the tax treatment of each method and provide a definitive answer to this important tax planning question.

Part 7 – Motoring Expenses

This part of the guide contains invaluable information for business owners who want to maximise tax relief on their motoring costs (including reclaiming VAT).

In Chapter 21, we explain the capital allowances that can be claimed when you buy motor vehicles, including the 100% tax deduction when you buy cars with low CO_2 emissions. We also explain how self-employed business owners can claim big catch-up tax deductions when they sell their cars.

Chapter 22 looks at vehicle running costs and explains how much you can claim for fuel, insurance, maintenance etc.

Small business owners can either claim tax relief on their actual motoring costs or use HMRC's fixed mileage rates. In Chapter 23 we use some examples to show which method produces the biggest tax saving.

Chapters 24 and 25 are all about maximising the amount of VAT you can recover on your motoring costs. Chapter 24 lists all the purchases that qualify: vans, motorbikes, accessories, repairs, parking costs, number plates etc.

When it comes to reclaiming VAT on your fuel you have two choices: reclaim VAT on your actual business mileage only or reclaim VAT on all your fuel and pay the Fuel Scale Charge. In Chapter 25 we reveal which method produces a bigger VAT refund.

If you drive a van you can recover over half the cost in tax relief, including a VAT refund and a 100% capital allowance. In Chapter 26 we reveal which vehicles qualify for the full monty of tax reliefs (it's not just Ford Transits!)

In Chapter 27 we provide a definitive answer to a very important tax planning question: Should I lease or buy my car?

Part 8 – Maximising Tax Relief on Borrowings

Chapter 28 explains how you can claim a bigger tax deduction for interest on borrowed money and how to avoid various mistakes that will reduce your tax relief.

In Chapter 29 we reveal how business owners can even make interest on a personal loan (eg a home mortgage) tax deductible.

Part 9 – Business Property

Chapter 30 will help you decide whether it is best to rent or buy premises for your business.

In Chapter 31 we explain the difference between property repairs and improvements. Repairs will generally save you more tax. We reveal how certain spending that increases the value of your property can be treated as a repair for tax purposes.

When you buy a commercial property you can claim immediate tax relief for the value of all the central heating, wiring, lighting and other 'integral features'. Chapter 32 tells you everything you need to know about this generous tax deduction.

In Chapter 33 we explain how you can accelerate tax relief on loan arrangement fees.

Part 10 – E-Commerce

Most businesses have an internet presence these days. In Chapter 34 we explain the rules for claiming tax relief on the various costs, including website development costs, domain names and online advertising.

Dedicated internet businesses can take advantage of other tax saving opportunities, including moving to a lower tax jurisdiction. We provide a brief summary in Chapter 35.

Part 11 – Year-End Tax Planning & Pro-active Accounting

In Chapter 36 we list the things you should do before the end of the tax year to reduce your business's tax bill. Normally this involves accelerating expenses and pushing income into the next tax year; sometimes it involves the opposite approach.

Another thing you may be able to do is change your business year-end itself! In Chapter 37 we explain how doing this could save you thousands of pounds in tax.

Chapter 38 explains how businesses that sell goods can maximise their tax deduction for Cost of Sales.

Chapter 39 explains how you can claim a bigger tax deduction for bad debts.

In Chapter 40 we explain what you must do to ensure that your accountant does their job correctly.

Part 12 – VAT

Most business owners hate VAT. In Chapter 41 we explain the basics and in Chapters 42 and 43 we look at various special schemes that could save your business thousands of pounds in VAT every year.

Part 13 – Capital Gains Tax

Business owners who cash in their chips are in a privileged position when it comes to Capital Gains Tax: they can pay just 10% tax. This is thanks to Entrepreneurs' Relief and in Chapter 44 we explain the rules.

In Chapter 45 we reveal how it is possible, in certain circumstances, to pay just 10% Capital Gains Tax when you sell an investment property by running a business out of it for a year.

Part 14 – Inheritance Tax

Business owners are also in a fortunate position when it comes to Inheritance Tax: they can completely avoid the grave robbers thanks to a special relief called business property relief. In Chapter 46 we explain how this relief works and in Chapter 47 we explain what you must do to protect it.

Part 15 – Other Important Tax Issues

In the final part of this guide, we look at some other important tax issues not covered elsewhere, including the voluntary cash accounting scheme for small businesses, which is covered in Chapter 48.

It is important that readers are aware of the potential benefits and drawbacks of this new accounting method and its impact on all of the other tax planning strategies contained in this guide.

Readers should note that, unless expressly stated to the contrary, it is assumed throughout the rest of the guide that the cash accounting scheme is not being used.

Chapter 49 looks at some of the most useful tax planning techniques available to avoid the High Income Child Benefit Charge on income between £50,000 and £60,000.

Finally, in Chapter 50 we take a look at the tax relief cap which places an annual limit on the total combined amount of Income Tax relief available under a number of different reliefs.

Chapter 2

How Much Tax Do Small Business Owners Pay?

Income Tax and National Insurance

Self-employed business owners pay Income Tax and National Insurance on their taxable profits.

For the 2016/17 tax year, ending on 5th April 2017, most self-employed individuals pay Income Tax as follows:

- 0%   on the first   £11,000   Personal allowance
- 20%   on the next   £32,000   Basic-rate band
- 40%   above   £43,000   Higher-rate threshold

Generally speaking, if you earn more than £43,000 you are a higher-rate taxpayer; if you earn less you are a basic-rate taxpayer.

The Income Tax paid by the self-employed is exactly the same as that paid by other taxpayers, such as salary earners. However, the National Insurance position is completely different.

For the current 2016/17 tax year, self-employed business owners usually pay Class 4 National Insurance as follows:

- 0%   on the first   £8,060
- 9%   on the next   £34,940
- 2%   above   £43,000

Those with earnings over the £5,965 small profits threshold also pay Class 2 National Insurance (£2.80 per week, £146 for the year).

Class 2 National Insurance will be abolished from April 2018 and the Government has been consulting on reforming Class 4 National Insurance.

Certain types of income are not subject to National Insurance, including interest from bank accounts (including business bank accounts), pensions and rental income.

Business Profits over £100,000

When your taxable income exceeds £100,000, your Income Tax personal allowance is gradually withdrawn. For every additional £1 you earn, 50p of your personal allowance is taken away.

What this means is that, when your income for 2016/17 reaches £122,000, your personal allowance will have completely disappeared. It also means that self-employed taxpayers who earn between £100,000 and £122,000 face a marginal tax rate of 62%.

Example
Caroline's sole trader business has generated taxable business profits of £100,000 so far during the current tax year. If she makes an extra £1 of profit she will pay an extra 42p of Income Tax and National Insurance.

She will also lose 50p of her Income Tax personal allowance, which means 50p of income that was tax free will now be taxed at 40%, resulting in extra tax of 20p. All in all she pays 62p in tax on her extra £1 of profit, so her marginal tax rate is 62%.

Business Profits over £150,000

Once your taxable business profits for 2016/17 exceed £150,000, you have to pay 45% Income Tax on any additional profits. This 'super tax' rate is officially known as the 'additional rate'.

Marginal Tax Rates

Putting all of the above Income Tax and National Insurance rates together, we can see that most self-employed business owners face the following combined marginal tax rates in 2016/17:

First £5,965	£0
£5,965 to £8,060	£146 (fixed cost)
£8,060 to £11,000	9%
£11,000 to £43,000	29%
£43,000 to £100,000	42%
£100,000 to £122,000	62%
£122,000 to £150,000	42%
Over £150,000	47%

Tax Planning with Marginal Tax Rates

If you know roughly how much taxable profit your business is likely to make, you can do some constructive tax planning:

Example 1
Alana is a sole trader and expects to make taxable profits of £45,000 during the current tax year. If she incurs an additional £1,000 of tax deductible expenditure, this will reduce her tax bill for the year by £420 (£1,000 x 42%).

Example 2
Shelly is a sole trader and expects to make taxable profits of £35,000 during the current tax year. If she incurs an additional £1,000 of tax deductible expenditure, this will reduce her tax bill for the year by £290 (£1,000 x 29%).

Example 1 continued
Alana expects her taxable profits to fall from £45,000 to around £30,000 during the next 2017/18 tax year. This means her marginal tax rate will fall from 42% to 29%. If she incurs £1,000 of tax deductible expenditure in 2016/17 she will save £420 in tax; if she spends the money in 2017/18 she will save £290 in tax. Alana should try to spend the money during the current tax year, rather than next year (assuming she can afford to).

Example 2 continued
Shelly expects her taxable profits to rise from £35,000 to £50,000 during the next 2017/18 tax year. This means her marginal tax rate will rise from 29% to 42%.

If she incurs £1,000 of tax deductible expenditure in 2016/17 she will save £290 in tax; if she spends the money in 2017/18 she will save £420 in tax. Shelly may want to consider postponing the expenditure until next year (assuming this is commercially feasible).

Total Tax Bills

A lot of tax planning uses these marginal tax rates and revolves around reducing the tax on the top slice of your income. You may also be interested to see the total tax paid by self-employed business owners at different profit levels. This is illustrated in the table below.

The final column is the average tax rate which is simply total tax divided by total income. So, for example, someone who earns £50,000 faces a *marginal tax rate* of 42% and can save £420 in tax by reducing their taxable income by £1,000. However, they don't pay 42% tax on all of their income, only the top slice. When you take into account personal allowances, basic-rate tax bands, etc, the average tax rate is 25%.

Total Tax 2016/17
Self-Employed Business Owners

Income	Income Tax	Class 2 NI	Class 4 NI	Total Tax	Average Tax Rate
£20,000	£1,800	£146	£1,075	£3,021	15%
£30,000	£3,800	£146	£1,975	£5,921	20%
£40,000	£5,800	£146	£2,875	£8,821	22%
£50,000	£9,200	£146	£3,285	£12,631	25%
£60,000	£13,200	£146	£3,485	£16,831	28%
£70,000	£17,200	£146	£3,685	£21,031	30%
£100,000	£29,200	£146	£4,285	£33,631	34%
£150,000	£53,600	£146	£5,285	£59,031	39%
£200,000	£76,100	£146	£6,285	£82,531	41%

Older Self Employed Taxpayers

Older self-employed taxpayers face a broadly similar tax burden to their younger counterparts, but there are a few differences:

- Taxpayers over state pension age are exempt from both Class 2 and Class 4 National Insurance.

- Married taxpayers, and those in civil partnerships, where one spouse or partner was born before 6th April 1935, may also be entitled to a married couples allowance yielding a tax saving of up to £835.50 for 2016/17.

Throughout this guide, unless expressly stated to the contrary, it is assumed for the purpose of all examples, tables, and other calculations, that the business owner is below state pension age and that none of the above differences therefore apply.

For a higher rate taxpayer over state pension age, the only significant difference which this makes is that their marginal tax rate will be 2% less.

Marriage Allowance

It is now possible to transfer 10% of your personal allowance to your spouse or civil partner (£1,100 during the current 2016/17 tax year). Unmarried couples are excluded.

Only basic-rate taxpayers can benefit from this tax break, so the potential tax saving is £220 (£1,100 x 20%).

Married couples can generally only benefit from this tax break if:

- One person earns less than £11,000 and is therefore wasting some of their personal allowance

- The other person earns less than £43,000 (i.e. is a basic-rate taxpayer)

Both individuals must have been born on or after 6 April 1935.

You have to register to use it:

www.gov.uk/marriage-allowance

Potential winners are married couples where one person does not work (e.g. full-time parents) or only has a part-time job.

Example

In 2016/17 Bill, a sole trader, earns profits of £30,000 and his wife Daphne earns £6,000 working part time. Daphne has £5,000 of unused personal allowance. She can transfer £1,100 of this to Bill which means Bill no longer has to pay tax on £1,100 of his income. This will save him £220 in tax (£1,100 x 20%).

In the chapters that follow, it is assumed in all examples and calculations that the marriage allowance does not apply.

The High Income Child Benefit Charge

An additional Income Tax charge is levied on the highest earner in any household where:

- Any member of the household has annual income in excess of £50,000, and
- Child Benefit is being claimed

The additional tax charge is equivalent to 1% of the Child Benefit claimed in the same tax year for every £100 by which the highest earner's income exceeds £50,000. Once the highest earner's income reaches £60,000, the whole of the Child Benefit will effectively have been withdrawn and the charge will have reached its maximum.

Self-employed taxpayers below state pension age who are affected by the charge in 2016/17 will have an overall effective marginal tax rate on income between £50,000 and £60,000 as follows:

No. of Qualifying Children	Effective Tax Rate
1 Child	53%
2 Children	60%
3 Children	67%
4 Children	74%
Each additional child	+7%

Anyone with more than seven qualifying children will be suffering an overall marginal tax rate in excess of 100%!

As an alternative to the Income Tax charge, the claimant can choose not to claim Child Benefit. This may be a simple choice for employed earners with high salaries but, for self-employed taxpayers, it is generally very difficult to know their overall income for the year in advance. Hence, many self-employed business owners with young children will be suffering the charge.

The highest earner's total annual income for the purpose of the charge is their 'adjusted net income'. This means taxable income less 'grossed up' gift aid and personal pension contributions, making these reliefs extremely valuable to individuals who are subject to the High Income Child Benefit Charge.

15

Example

Peter makes a business profit of £60,000 for the year ending 31ˢᵗ December 2016. This is treated as taxable income for the 2016/17 tax year. He has no other taxable income for the year. His wife, Jenna, has taxable income of less than £50,000.

Peter and Jenna have four children aged under 16, so Jenna is entitled to claim a total of £3,214 in Child Benefit for 2016/17. As things stand, this entire sum will be clawed back from Peter by way of the High Income Child Benefit Charge.

In March 2017, however, Peter makes a personal pension contribution of £8,000. For tax purposes, this is treated as a 'gross' contribution of £10,000, with basic rate tax relief at 20% having been given at source.

Peter's 'gross' pension contribution reduces his 'adjusted net income' to £50,000 (£60,000 - £10,000), so he now avoids the High Income Child Benefit Charge for 2016/17.

Peter's higher rate tax relief on the contribution will also save a further £2,000 in Income Tax (£10,000 x 40% = £4,000 LESS £2,000 relief already given at source = £2,000).

Hence, Peter's cash contribution of £8,000 will save him a total of £5,214 (£3,214 + £2,000) in Income Tax. Looked at another way, Peter has managed to put £10,000 into his pension pot at a net cost of just £2,786 (£8,000 - £5,214).

We will look at some other ways of avoiding, or at least mitigating, the High Income Child Benefit Charge in Chapter 49.

In all other chapters of this guide, unless expressly stated to the contrary, it is assumed for the purpose of all examples, tables, and other calculations, that the High Income Child Benefit Charge does not apply.

However, for those who are affected, any tax planning measures which reduce taxable income falling into the band from £50,000 to £60,000, will be of even greater value.

Interest Income

A new personal savings allowance has been introduced with effect from 6th April 2016. It introduces a 0% tax rate (the savings nil rate) for up to £1,000 of interest income if you're a basic-rate taxpayer and up to £500 if you're a higher-rate taxpayer. Additional-rate taxpayers do not receive this new allowance.

The personal savings allowance will be useful for self-employed business owners who hold a significant amount of cash.

Income that falls within your savings allowance will still count towards your basic-rate or higher-rate limit and may therefore affect the level of savings allowance you're entitled to and the rate of tax payable on any savings income you receive in excess of this allowance.

As part of this change, the automatic deduction of 20% Income Tax by banks and building societies on non-ISA savings has been halted. Any tax which still remains due on bank and building society interest will now be collected through self-assessment. (HMRC may also attempt to collect some of this tax through the PAYE system in some cases.)

Interest from peer-to-peer loans can also be sheltered from tax thanks to the new personal savings allowance.

Of course, most individuals can shelter all of their interest income from tax by putting their money in a cash ISA. However, the new personal savings allowance may give you the freedom to put your savings into an account that pays the most competitive interest rate, which may not be a cash ISA. It may also free up more of your annual ISA allowance to invest in shares and equity funds, if that's what you prefer to do.

The £5,000 Starting Rate Band

There is also a 0% starting rate for up to £5,000 of interest income, however in most cases only those on low incomes can use it.

You can only benefit from the 0% starting rate if your *non-savings income* does not exceed £16,000 (£11,000 personal allowance plus

£5,000 starting rate band). Your non-savings income typically includes your self-employment profits, salary income, rental income and pensions but does not include your dividends.

Most readers probably cannot use the 0% starting rate because they will have more than £16,000 of non-savings income. You may, however, be able to benefit from the new personal savings allowance (discussed above).

Example

Denise has a self-employment profit of £16,000 and interest income of £2,000. The first £11,000 of her self-employment profit is tax free and the remaining £5,000 is taxed at 20%. The £5,000 of taxable non-savings income effectively "eats up" her £5,000 starting rate band. She is, however, entitled to a £1,000 savings allowance which shelters £1,000 of her interest income from tax. The remaining £1,000 of interest income will be taxed at 20%.

It is important to point out that the 0% starting rate band is not given in addition to your basic-rate band (£32,000 in 2016/17). Instead it is part of the basic-rate band.

Future Income Tax Changes

Income Tax Rates and Thresholds

The Government has stated that Income Tax will be levied as follows next year (2017/18):

		2017/18	
0%	on the first	£11,500	Personal allowance
20%	on the next	£33,500	Basic-rate band
40%	above	£45,000	Higher-rate threshold

The Government has also committed to raising the personal allowance to at least £12,500 by 2020/21 and then keeping it equivalent to working at least 30 hours a week on the national minimum wage.

The Government has also committed to raising the higher-rate threshold to at least £50,000 by 2020/21.

The Tax Lock

Legislation has been introduced to fix the maximum Income Tax rates as follows:

- Basic rate   20%
- Higher rate   40%
- Additional rate   45%

The tax lock will apply to the 2016/17 to 2019/20 tax years.

It will apply to all savings income received by UK taxpayers and to earned income received by taxpayers in England, Wales and Northern Ireland. It does not apply to earned income received by Scottish taxpayers, as the rates applying to this income are now set by the Scottish Parliament.

Legislation has been introduced preventing increases in the Class 1 National Insurance rates payable by employers and employees. However, no such commitment was made to protect self-employed business owners from paying more Class 4 National Insurance.

The Government has also legislated to keep the standard VAT rate at 20% and the reduced rate at 5% and to prevent items being removed from the list of items that qualify for the reduced and zero VAT rates.

Scottish Income Tax

The Scottish Rate of Income Tax (SRIT) came into force on 6 April 2016, although it does not affect the amount of Income Tax paid by people living in Scotland. This is because, for 2016/17, the Scottish Government has decided to keep Scottish tax rates the same as the rates paid by other UK taxpayers.

The Scottish Parliament has the power to tax salaries, self-employment income, rental income and pensions. It does not have the power to tax savings and dividend income.

The UK Parliament also has the power to set the personal allowance. National Insurance and most other taxes, including Corporation Tax, Capital Gains Tax and Inheritance Tax, remain the preserve of the UK Government.

Someone is a Scottish taxpayer if their sole or main place of residence is in Scotland.

For example, someone who rents a flat in London where they work during the week will probably be treated as a Scottish taxpayer if their spouse and children live in the family home in Edinburgh and most of their friends and other social links are also in Edinburgh.

In some cases it may be much more difficult to establish where the main residence is located.

Where no close connection to Scotland can be identified (for example, because it is not possible to establish the person's main place of residence), Scottish taxpayer status will be determined through day counting.

At present those who split their lives between Scotland and the rest of the UK don't have much to gain or lose by being classified as Scottish or UK taxpayers.

However, this could all change from next year when the Scottish Government obtains greater tax powers.

More Tax Changes for Scots in the Pipeline

Following the Scottish independence referendum, the Smith Commission recommended giving the Scottish Parliament greater tax powers. These recommendations were included in the Scotland Bill and will take effect from April 2017.

The Scottish Government will have complete power to set Income Tax rates and thresholds. This means it will be able to put up the top rate of tax without increasing the basic rate or higher rate and change the thresholds where the various tax rates kick in. It will also be able to create entirely new Income Tax bands and rates.

The Scottish Government will not, however, have the power to alter the tax treatment of savings income and dividend income. It also cannot change the personal allowance, although effectively it can do this by introducing a new 0% tax bracket.

In March 2016 the Scottish Government announced that it will not increase the basic rate or higher rate in 2017/18. Astonishingly it will even keep the additional rate at 45% (apparently the Scottish Government fears that wealthy Scots would simply go south if they were taxed more heavily).

That's the good news. The bad news is that, unlike the rest of the UK, the higher-rate threshold will NOT be increased to £45,000 next year and ultimately to £50,000. Instead it will only be increased in line with inflation.

Other Taxes Paid by the Self Employed

The main focus of this guide is helping sole traders and partnerships pay less Income Tax and National Insurance on their business profits. However, there are other taxes that may have to be paid and are covered in this guide:

- Employer's National Insurance when you take on employees (See Chapter 7)

- VAT if your business is VAT registered (See Part 12, as well as Chapters 24 and 25 covering VAT relief on motoring costs).

- Capital Gains Tax when you sell your business or any business assets (covered in Chapters 44 and 45).

- Inheritance Tax (covered in Chapters 46 and 47).

Part 1

Working from Home

Chapter 3

How to Claim a Big Home Office Tax Deduction

Many businesses start in a spare bedroom or on the dining room table. Even when they're well established, most business owners work from home at least part of the time, for example during the evening or on weekends.

Working from home means you can claim part of your household costs for tax purposes.

But who can claim, how much and which costs?

Almost everyone in business can make some claim for 'use of home'. We don't know any business owner who doesn't at least take some paperwork home or make business calls from home.

Imagine you're a sole trader running a small garage. You need to renew your business premises insurance. You take the proposal form home to complete after work. You've just used your home for business and you are entitled to make a claim.

It constantly amazes us how many people think they're not entitled to the 'use of home' deduction: there are so many popular misconceptions about it.

Many people think they can't claim because they're already claiming for an office, a shop, or other business premises. Not true!

Although the amount of the claim is likely to be less, a 'use of home' claim is still possible as long as some work is carried out at home.

(It's also worth noting that, if you have two or more homes, you can make claims in respect of any business use of any of them.)

Business partners need to ensure the costs go through their firm's accounts. This will need the other partners to agree the claim, but this doesn't stop a claim from being made.

How Much Can You Claim?

Claims should be based on the proportionate use of the property for business. The main factors to consider are *time* and *space*: how much space is set aside for business use and how much time is spent on business.

There are many possible methods for calculating the business proportion. In practice, the most popular method is to simply take the number of rooms used for business as a proportion of the total number of rooms in the house. Hallways, bathrooms and kitchens are excluded from the calculation.

Example

Billie designs rose gardens and uses a room in his house as his office. The house also has two bedrooms, a living room, a dining room, two bathrooms and a kitchen.

We can ignore the bathrooms and the kitchen, so this leaves five rooms for the purpose of our calculation, meaning that Billie can claim one fifth of his household costs.

So, if Billie's annual household costs amount to £20,000 and he uses the office room exclusively for business, this entitles him to claim a tax deduction of £4,000.

What Expenses Can Be Claimed?

Most people don't realise how many costs can be claimed if they work from home. A self-employed person working from home is entitled to claim a proportion of most household costs, including:

- Mortgage interest or rent
- Council tax
- Water rates
- Repairs and maintenance
- Building and contents insurance
- Electricity
- Gas, oil or other heating costs
- Cleaning

Telephone and internet costs may also be claimed, where relevant, although this tends to form a separate claim as the business element of these costs is usually a far higher proportion than for other household costs.

A proportion of general repairs and maintenance costs relating to the whole property, such as roof repairs or gas maintenance costs may be claimed.

Costs which are specific to an area used for work may be claimed in full – subject to any reduction required for partial private use of that area.

Redecorating a study used for work would be an allowable cost, for example. The flipside of this is that any costs specific to a wholly non-work area may not be claimed at all.

Capital allowances may also be claimed on any furniture and equipment used for business, with immediate 100% relief usually available thanks to the annual investment allowance, subject to a reduction for any private use. (See Chapter 16 for more information on the annual investment allowance.)

Floor Space Instead of Rooms

In the earlier example with Billie the claim was based on the number of rooms used for business purposes.

This method is nice and simple, but it is always worth considering whether another method might yield a better result. What if Billie's design work requires a lot of space and the room he uses is actually the largest in the house?

In this case, it would be better if Billie did his calculation based on floor space, as this would produce a greater deduction for him.

More Complex Claims

There is an almost infinite range of other factors you might consider.

Suppose Billie's office requires specialised lighting which consumes a lot of electricity – he might be able to claim a higher proportion of his electricity bills.

Billie might argue that his work equipment is highly valuable and he should therefore claim a higher proportion of his contents insurance.

(In fact, such equipment may sometimes need a separate policy – if so, this would be allowed in full, but with no deduction allowed for Billie's 'normal' contents insurance.)

Take care when isolating individual costs in this way though. Moving away from the simple method is like opening Pandora's Box; you will need to be consistent and there may be other elements to your claim which go the other way, leaving you worse off than when you started.

In particular, HM Revenue and Customs (HMRC) takes the view that 'fixed' annual costs such as mortgage interest, council tax and insurance need to be allocated on the basis that a room is available for private use whenever it isn't being used for business.

This method creates a great deal of complexity and is not widely followed in practice when there is extensive business use of the home. It may, however, be appropriate to use this method where the business use is less extensive and we will look at this situation later in this chapter.

Wasted Space

It may be worth thinking about the impact on your claim of a room with little or no use of any kind.

Let's suppose that Billie never uses his dining room. The room's mere existence means he is claiming just one fifth of his household costs. Arguably, if the room is never used, he might justifiably claim a quarter instead.

Better still, Billie should start using the dining room for business. Then he could claim up to two fifths of his household costs (depending on how much he uses the room).

Using a room for business can take many forms – completing paperwork, taking business calls, meeting customers, storing files or other business items – even just sitting there thinking about your business.

Reduce Your Claim and Save CGT

When there is some private use of a room used for business, you will need to restrict your home office claim.

For example, let's say once a week, Billie has some friends round for a game of poker and they use his office. They play for about four hours each week. Billie works in his office for 46 hours a week on average, so his business use amounts to 46/50ths, or 92%.

With total annual household costs of £20,000 and five rooms to be taken into account, this means that Billie may now claim a deduction of £3,680 (£20,000 x 1/5 x 92%).

"Why don't they play cards in the dining room?" you may ask. One possible reason is that Billie wants to protect his Capital Gains Tax (CGT) exemption.

The CGT exemption which you usually get when you sell your home is restricted if part of the house has been used exclusively for business.

Fortunately, as long as there is some private use of each room in the house, no matter how small, your CGT relief is safe.

In fact, you can counter-balance that small element of private use of your 'work room' with a small element of business use in another room, thus restoring your Income Tax deduction to its previous level with no loss of CGT relief.

For example, if Billie used his dining room for business 8% of the time, his total claim would be restored to the original one fifth. In cases like this, it is wise to make a note of the logic behind your claim in case of any later enquiries.

Time-Based Claims

For smaller properties, looking at floor space or number of rooms may be unsuitable and it will often make more sense to make claims on a time basis instead.

Example
Donna is a self-employed web designer. She works at home in her small one bedroom flat. Because her flat is so small, Donna is effectively using the whole flat for business when she is working. Conversely, of course, when she isn't working, she is using the whole flat privately.

In this case, we could use what I call the 'work, rest and play' principle - assuming that Donna spends an equal amount of time on each, she should claim one third of her household costs.

Many self-employed people work more than a third of the time, so a greater claim will sometimes be justified.

Since HMRC staff are not self-employed, it may be wise to retain some evidence of your actual working hours in order to convince them of this!

Part-Timers

Those who work from home only part of the time, such as at evenings and weekends, will need to reduce their claim accordingly.

All of the methods for allocating household costs described above remain available, but a further reduction in the claim must be applied to reflect the part-time nature of the business use of part of the home.

Establishing this reduction needs to be considered on a case by case basis. The key watchword to remember is: be reasonable!

Let's say, for example, that you use your dining room for business purposes around 20 hours each week, but the room is also used privately (for meals, the children doing their homework, etc) around 30 hours each week. So, 40% of the room's total usage is business use.

Let's also say that there are five other rooms which we need to take into account (excluding hallways, bathrooms and kitchen, as usual) and your total annual household costs are £18,000.

In this case, it would seem reasonable for you to claim £1,200 (£18,000 x 1/6 x 40%) in respect of business use of your home.

As your dining room is used quite extensively (50 hours per week in total), it does not seem necessary, in this case, to look at 'fixed' costs like council tax and mortgage interest, differently to 'variable' costs like electricity.

Let's look at another example, however.

Example
Freema is a self-employed freelance medical consultant and she does some occasional work at home amounting to around three hours per week on average.

Based on the usual test, her flat has three rooms to be taken into account, including the spare bedroom which she only uses for work and for the occasional guest. She has very few guests, so her business use of the spare room amounts to 90% of the room's total usage.

Freema's total annual household costs amount to £12,000.

If we used our usual formula, this would produce a claim of £3,600 (£12,000 x 1/3 x 90%).

However, taking a reasonable view, we see that this amounts to a rather ridiculous and unsustainable claim of over £23 per hour of business use.

Hence, in this case, it seems reasonable to apply HMRC's approach, whereby 'fixed' costs are allocated on the basis of how much time the room is actually used for business as a proportion of how much time the room is available for use.

Let's say that Freema has £10,000 of 'fixed' costs and £2,000 of variable costs. There are 168 hours in a week, but it is reasonable to assume that a room is only available for use 16 hours per day, or 112 hours per week. Freema's tax deduction is therefore calculated as follows:

| Fixed costs: | £10,000 x 1/3 x 3/112 | £89 |
| Variable costs: | £2,000 x 1/3 x 90% | £600 |

| Total claim: | | £689 |

This is a much more reasonable and sensible claim in Freema's case.

For the purpose of these types of calculations, fixed costs would include:

- Mortgage interest or rent
- Council tax
- Water rates (but not if the supply is metered)
- Building and contents insurance

Minimal Use

For cases where there is only minimal business use of the home, HMRC's instructions suggest that claims of up to £2 a week (or £104 a year) will be acceptable, although some actual business use of the home is required, even if only very small.

This is particularly useful for those with only a small amount of work to do at home, such as a landlord with just one rental property.

It isn't much, but it saves the effort of doing any more complex calculations.

It is worth noting that the £2 per week rate has been included in HMRC's manuals relating to self-employed business income for some time. Meanwhile, the rate allowed to employees working from home has been increased to £4 per week (or £208 a year) and some commentators believe that it is reasonable to assume that HMRC will now allow this same rate for self-employed business owners rather than the £2 per week rate shown in the business income manual. Sadly, the position here is not entirely clear!

Flat Rate Deductions

From 2013/14 onwards, a new system of flat rate deductions for business use of the taxpayer's home is available for trading businesses.

The flat rate deductions are an alternative method which is available **instead of** the proportionate calculation discussed above.

The amount of the deduction is calculated on a monthly basis according to the number of hours spent wholly and exclusively working on business matters. The rates applying are:

Hours worked in the month	Deduction allowed for the month
25 to 50	£10
51 to 100	£18
101 or more	£26

Example
Clara runs a small trading business from her home. She draws up accounts to 31ˢᵗ March each year. From April to July 2016 she spends 40 hours per month working at home. She takes a holiday in August and does no work at home. She has some catching up to do in September and spends 110 hours working at home that month. She then spends around 55 hours per month working at home from October 2016 to March 2017 – except in December when she only manages to work about 20 hours.

If Clara chooses to use the flat rate deduction for her 'use of home', she will be able to claim:

4 months at £10 = £40   (April to July)
1 month at £26 = £26   (September)
5 months at £18 = £90   (October, November, January to March)
2 months at £0 = £0   (August and December)
Total claim: £156

Laughingly, this incredibly complex calculation, which produces a deduction of a mere £156 in this case, is brought to us under a regime called 'Simplified Expenses'!

The new flat rate deductions are not exactly generous, so I find it difficult to believe that many business owners working from home will want to use them anyway.

Anyone who feels that it is not worthwhile performing complex calculations to arrive at a suitable proportion of household expenses can still claim the simple deduction of £2 per week described above.

In our last example, Clara could have claimed a 'use of home' deduction of £104 for the year ending 31st March 2017 without having to carry out **any** calculations (some people would argue she could claim £208 in fact: for the reasons explained above).

She would almost certainly be better off carrying out a proper calculation and claiming a suitable proportion of her actual household running costs.

Chapter 4

Part-time Business, Special Tax Rules

Many people start out with a part-time business for various reasons:

- You may have a full-time job and start a sideline business

- You may see a part-time business as an easier way to make the transition to self-employment

- You may already have an existing business in a different field, or

- You may even be turning your hobby into a business.

Recent years have also seen the growth of the online business, which is often run from home on a part-time basis.

So, what are the tax issues that you need to consider when you start a little 'something on the side'?

What's the Difference?

As far as the tax system is concerned, there are very few differences between a part-time business and a full-time one.

The major differences come in the areas of loss relief and National Insurance and we will look at these a little later.

As far as calculating profits and tax deductions is concerned, there is really very little difference.

Do You Have a Business?

The first step, however, is to determine whether you actually have a business in the first place. Although a hobby or other activity can evolve into a business, it can be difficult to tell exactly when this happens. Some old case law gives us six tests to indicate when a business exists:

i) The activity is a 'serious undertaking earnestly pursued' or a 'serious occupation'.

ii) The activity is 'an occupation or function actively pursued with reasonable or recognisable continuity'.

iii) The activity has 'a certain measure of substance as measured by the value of supplies made'.

iv) The activity is 'conducted in a regular manner and on sound and recognised business principles'.

v) The activity is 'predominantly concerned with the making of supplies to consumers'.

vi) The goods or services supplied 'are of a kind which, subject to differences in detail, are commonly made by those who seek to profit by them'.

Where some or all of the above tests are met, you probably have a business. The language of the tests is a bit 'legalese' though, so what do they actually mean?

To me, the tests can be summed up by saying that something which you do on a regular basis, in an organised manner, with the intention of realising a profit, is a business.

If you do have a business, it will usually be a trade, but there are some important exceptions to this. For example, a supply of services may sometimes be a profession rather than a trade (although there is very little difference in the tax treatment).

Property rental businesses have their own special rules and, whilst it can be a business, investing on the stock market will almost never be regarded as a trade.

For the rest of this chapter, I will assume that your part-time business is a trade. Before I move on though, I should point out that, just because you do not have a business, this does not mean that any profits or gains you make are not taxable. Although there are many exemptions which can apply (like selling your house or car), any time you make money on something, there is a good chance that it is taxable!

Property & Trading Income Allowances

Having said this, two new allowances of £1,000 each will be available to exempt small amounts or property income or trading income from 2017/18 onwards.

Individuals with property income or trading income below the level of the allowance will no longer need to declare or pay tax on that income.

Where the gross income exceeds the £1,000 allowance, the individual will be able to either deduct expenses as normal, or deduct the allowance from the gross income.

This exemption has been introduced to help those who earn small amounts of income from websites like eBay or Airbnb.

Why Does Having a Business Matter?

The good thing about having a business, as opposed to some sort of casual, windfall, income, is the fact that you can claim deductions against your business income.

The principles here are the same as for any full-time business and hence, as well as your direct business costs, you will be able to claim all the usual things like premises costs, motor expenses, travel and subsistence, legal and professional fees, etc: as long as the costs are incurred for the purposes of the business.

For the part-time business owner, the only 'business premises' they have will often be their own home. This means that they are entitled to claim a proportion of all their household running costs, including: mortgage interest, council tax, insurance, repairs, gas, electricity and other utilities.

But Size Doesn't Matter

It doesn't matter if it only takes you an hour a week to run your business: as long as you have a business, you are entitled to claim tax deductions under the same rules as everyone else.

One thing you should bear in mind, though, is that it naturally follows that, if your business is only part-time, you will generally only be able to claim a lower level of expenses than a full-time business, particularly when it comes to things like motor expenses and 'use of home'.

For example, a 'use of home' claim equal to 25% of your household running costs might be appropriate for a full-time business, but would be hard to justify if you only spend five hours a week on your business!

Each case has to be decided on its own merits, but the key thing to remember is that you need to restrict your claims to something which is reasonable under the circumstances.

Loss Relief

Where a part-time trading business gives rise to losses, the general rule is that these can be set off against the proprietor's other income or capital gains for the same tax year or the previous one.

This is another advantage of having a business rather than casual income and it means that many part-time traders are able to claim repayments of tax paid under PAYE on employment income, or else reduce the tax due under self-assessment on other sources of income.

There are, however, two areas of difficulty in claiming loss relief for part-time businesses.

The first problem is that, when it comes to part-time businesses, HMRC have a tendency to want to 'have their cake and eat it'. If the business makes a profit, HMRC will want to tax it, if it makes a loss, they may claim that it is actually just a hobby and thus deny any loss relief.

When a loss arises, therefore, it is important to be able to point to the six tests which we looked at earlier and to show that your business meets at least some of them. Most importantly, however, you need to be able to show that you are in business with the intention of making a profit: you cannot claim relief for a loss unless you were trying to make a profit.

There are many ways to demonstrate your intention to make a profit and the facts of the case will often speak for themselves. One of the best defences is to have a business plan which shows not only that you hope to make a profit, but also how!

The other problem for part-timers is that loss relief is restricted to a maximum of just £25,000 in each tax year where you spend an average of less than ten hours per week working in the business. This covers both part-time sole traders and part-time business partners and the £25,000 limit applies to the total losses from all your part-time businesses.

This rule was brought in a few years ago as an anti-avoidance measure aimed at investment partnerships but, sadly, it also catches many genuine part-time businesses. The second best way to get around it is to make sure that you work at least ten hours per week in the business. If you are close to this threshold, it may be worth keeping time records to demonstrate that you are working more than the required minimum number of hours.

The best way to avoid this rule though is to make a profit!

It is also worth noting that further restrictions in this type of loss relief for all businesses apply from 2013/14 onwards.

National Insurance for Part-Timers

The downside to having a business is that you will generally have to pay National Insurance. There are some important exceptions to be aware of though. You don't usually have to pay National Insurance if:

- You are over state pension age at the beginning of the tax year

- You are under 16 at the end of the tax year

- Your business is not a trade or profession

You can also claim exemption from National Insurance if your annual business profits are less than the 'small profits threshold' (£5,965 for 2016/17).

If you have more than one trading business, either as a sole trader or as a partner, you will only pay one Class 2 National Insurance contribution of £2.80 per week and your total profits will simply be added together to calculate your Class 4 liability.

Employment & Self Employment Income

The real complication comes when you have both employment and self-employment income and each of them amount to more than the National Insurance 'primary threshold' (£8,060 for 2016/17). In this situation, you will be liable for Class 1 National Insurance on your employment income and both Class 2 and Class 4 on your self-employment profits.

Where your total income from both sources amounts to more than the sum of the upper earnings limit (£43,000 for 2016/17) and the primary threshold, you may effectively 'overpay' National Insurance – i.e. you may pay more than you are required to by law.

You cannot simply reduce the amount that you pay: you will either have to put in a claim for exemption or make a repayment claim later.

Part 2

How Your Family Can Help You Save Tax

Chapter 5

How a Spouse or Partner Can Help You Save Tax

Transferring part of your income to your spouse or partner can save a higher-rate taxpayer up to £10,800 a year in Income Tax at current rates.

Sadly, not everyone has the freedom to 'transfer' their income easily, but most business owners do have some scope to effectively transfer part of their own income to their spouse or partner.

Furthermore, most of this type of planning works whether you're married or not. For the rest of this chapter, I will therefore just refer to 'partners' to cover husbands, wives, civil partners and unmarried partners alike.

Salaries

If your partner works in your business, you can pay them a salary.

Many business owners' partners contribute to the business on a part-time basis, even when they have a job of their own. The partner might help with the paperwork, take business telephone calls, clean overalls or other workwear, help with purchasing supplies, organise travel arrangements, or carry out any number of tasks associated with the business.

Any of these tasks will justify a salary payment (except for entertaining customers, which HMRC doesn't generally accept as 'work').

A salary of up to £8,060 can usually be paid in the current 2016/17 tax year without incurring any PAYE or National Insurance costs. At current rates, this would save a higher-rate taxpayer sole trader or business partner £3,385 in tax and National Insurance.

In fact, if we consider the top marginal tax rate of 62% which we examined in Chapter 2, some business owners could save up to £4,997 by paying this level of salary to their partner.

There are a few flies to watch out for in this ointment, however.

The most important point is that you can only get a deduction from your business profits in respect of your partner's salary if the payment to them is justified by the work that they do.

Furthermore, you must actually pay the salary to your partner. There is no automatic deduction just for having a partner. (Even if some might argue that there should be!)

If a payment of £8,060 isn't justified, a smaller payment should be made instead. Even a salary of just £2,000 could save you up to £1,240.

National Insurance will generally be payable on any salary payments in excess of £672 per month (or £155 per week). Any salary should therefore be paid on a regular basis and not in one lump sum.

You need to treat your partner like any other employee for all payroll purposes. Amongst other things, this means that you will have to be registered as an employer with HMRC before any salary payments can be made and you will have to apply any PAYE code issued for your partner by HMRC and operate the notoriously burdensome 'RTI' (real time information) procedures for payroll purposes.

If your partner has any other employment income, you will probably have to deduct basic rate Income Tax from their salary. This reduces the overall saving, but will still be worthwhile in most cases, as we will see below.

Some people feel that formally operating the PAYE system for a partner whose total income does not exceed the £8,060 National Insurance threshold is a piece of pointless red tape, but it has its benefits.

Any payment to a partner in excess of £112 per week will enhance their state pension entitlement - but only if you observe all the PAYE formalities. Plus, it's a legal requirement anyway.

When Does a Partner's Salary Save Tax?

The best savings naturally arise when the partner has no other income.

If the partner is a basic rate taxpayer, the saving will be smaller but still worthwhile. It now becomes a case of comparing the business owner's marginal tax rate with their partner's.

Remember that a sole trader or business partner will be paying National Insurance on their profits as well as Income Tax, but their employee partner can receive up to £8,060 free from National Insurance regardless of their income level.

A business owner paying higher rate tax will therefore still save a total of between 22% and 42% on a salary of up to £8,060 paid to a basic rate taxpayer partner - that's a maximum saving of between £1,773 and £3,385.

Even a business owner paying basic rate Income Tax can still save 9% National Insurance.

Too Much of a Good Thing?

Once you start to pay your partner more than £8,060, they will start to suffer employee's National Insurance at 12% on the excess.

And once their salary exceeds £8,112 you may also start to incur employer's National Insurance at 13.8%, unless your partner's salary is covered by the £3,000 employment allowance (see Chapter 7) or the exemption for under 21s and apprentices under 25 who are basic-rate taxpayers.

Surprisingly, there are still many cases where further salary payments will save tax overall.

Firstly, any payment which is covered by your partner's Income Tax personal allowance will usually be worthwhile. Subject to any other income they have, this could be up to £11,000 in 2016/17.

For higher rate taxpayer sole traders and business partners, any salary payment to a basic rate taxpayer partner will generally continue to save tax.

Take care not to pay too much, however. If your partner's salary takes their total income over the higher rate tax threshold (currently £43,000), or reduces your income below it, the salary will actually start to cost you extra tax.

Example
Colin runs a small bakery as a sole trader and expects to make a profit of £60,000 this year. His partner Bonnie has a part-time job as a secretary, earning £11,000, but also helps Colin in the bakery.

Colin pays Bonnie a salary of £15,922. She pays Income Tax at 20% on this plus National Insurance at 12% on the amount over £8,060 – a total of £4,127. Colin also has to pay National Insurance at 13.8% on the amount over £8,112. This amounts to £1,078, bringing the total tax cost of Bonnie's salary to £5,205.

Bonnie's salary and the employer's National Insurance paid by Colin amount to a total of £17,000 which is deductible from Colin's business profits, saving him tax at 42%, or £7,140. Overall, Bonnie's salary saves the couple a net sum of £1,935. (The first £8,060 saved them £1,773 and the rest produced a marginal additional saving of £162.)

BUT if Colin paid Bonnie another £1,000, it would cost a total of £458 in Income Tax and National Insurance whilst only saving Colin a further £330 on his own tax bill – an overall net cost of £128, or 12.8% of the additional salary.

As we can see, you can pay too much salary to your partner.

In the above example, I assumed that the employment allowance (see Chapter 7) was not available to exempt Colin from employer's National Insurance on Bonnie's salary. Let's return to the example and see what impact the allowance would have had if it had been available.

Example Part 2
Colin has no other employees apart from Bonnie and realises that the employer's allowance is available to exempt him from up to £3,000 employer's National Insurance on Bonnie's salary. He therefore increases her salary to £17,000. Bonnie now suffers a total of £4,473 in Income Tax and National Insurance, but Colin is exempt from any employer's National Insurance liability. Colin continues to make the same 42% tax saving of £7,140, which now leaves the couple £2,667 better off overall.

As we can see, the employer's allowance leads to a considerable increase in the potential saving on a salary payment made by a higher rate taxpayer to their basic rate taxpayer partner.

Where there are no other employees, the employer's allowance could exempt the employer from National Insurance on a salary of up to £29,851.

However, it remains important to limit the salary so that neither the employee becomes a higher rate taxpayer nor the employer becomes a basic rate taxpayer.

Partners in Partnership

Under the right circumstances, you can save a lot more tax by making your partner at home your partner at work too (i.e. making your life partner your business partner).

This has some very important legal implications which should be considered, some (but not all) of which can be resolved by using a Limited Liability Partnership.

This approach can be much more tax efficient because the National Insurance position for a business partner is much better than for an employee. Instead of employee's National Insurance at 12% and employer's at 13.8%, your partner will only pay Class 4 at 9% (plus £2.80 a week in Class 2).

For example, if Colin gave Bonnie a one third partnership share, the couple would save a total of £2,789 instead of the maximum saving of £1,935 achieved with a salary (where the employer's allowance is not available).

Furthermore, using this method, it would not matter that Colin's income had been reduced below the higher rate tax threshold – as long as Bonnie's was not increased above it!

Savings for High Earners

For those business owners facing marginal tax rates of 47% or 62% on their business profits, even a salary paid to a higher rate taxpayer partner could save tax.

Example

Ace anticipates making a profit of £110,000 for her accounting period ending 31ˢᵗ March 2017. Her husband Sylvester, who works as an accountant, estimates that this will give her a tax bill of £39,830.

Sylvester has always helped Ace with her business but, as he already has a salary of £50,000 from his main job, the couple could never see any point in Ace paying him another salary.

This year, however, Ace pays Sylvester a salary of £8,060. As he is a higher rate taxpayer, he will have to pay £3,224 in Income Tax but, since his main employment is not connected with Ace's business, there will be no National Insurance to pay.

Ace's business profits will be reduced to £101,940 and Sylvester estimates that this will now give her a tax bill of £34,833. She saves £4,997 and the couple are £1,773 better off overall.

Even if Ace's profits actually turn out to be just outside the 62% marginal rate band (income from £100,000 to £122,000), Sylvester's salary will still give them a small National Insurance saving, so there's usually no harm in trying this technique even if you're not quite sure where you stand.

On the other hand, if you're more certain about your profit levels, you may want to pay your partner even more. Where your marginal personal tax rate is 62%, any salary payment to your partner will save tax overall unless and until it takes them into the same marginal tax rate band.

Where your marginal tax rate is 47% (income over £150,000), a salary in excess of £8,112 paid to a higher rate taxpayer partner will not generally be beneficial – except to the extent that the employer's allowance is available to exempt you from any employer's National Insurance liability.

Your partner may need to reclaim any additional employee's National Insurance which they suffer on their salary from you in these cases.

Older Couples

Throughout this chapter I have assumed that both the business owner and their partner are below state pension age.

Where the business owner is over state pension age, the savings on any payment to their partner will be less because the business owner will not be paying Class 4 National Insurance.

Conversely, where the owner's partner is over state pension age, the savings on any salary payment will be greater because the partner will not suffer any employee's National Insurance. The owner will, however, still be liable for employer's National Insurance on any payments over £8,112 (unless the £3,000 employer's allowance is available).

Similarly, where a partner over state pension age becomes a business partner, they will not suffer any Class 2 or Class 4 National Insurance on their profit share.

These factors should be taken into account in planning salary payments or other tax saving strategies when either or both partners are over state pension age.

Compulsory Pension Contributions

Under the auto-enrolment regime, many businesses now have to make compulsory pension contributions on behalf of their employees. The regime does not yet apply to all small businesses, but will be extended to almost all businesses in the near future.

The tax planning in this chapter takes no account of the cost of compulsory pension contributions, nor the administrative cost of setting up a suitable scheme.

Where the partner to whom any salary is paid receives no more than £10,000, or chooses to opt out of the auto-enrolment regime, there will be no costs arising. In other cases, however, some costs are likely to arise.

We will look at the auto-enrolment regime in more detail in Chapter 10.

Chapter 6

Employing Children and Going into Business with Them

Children can place an enormous strain on your finances. So how about turning the tables and seeing what tax savings your children can generate for you?

Employing Children

Paying salaries to your children is a good way to reduce your taxable profits but which children can you legally employ?

With some limited exceptions for specific jobs (e.g. acting or modelling), it is generally illegal to employ children under 13. This will rule out most businesses from employing very young children, although there will be exceptions. The position for 13-year olds depends on local by-laws. Some areas allow them to do limited work, some allow them to do the same work as a 14-year-old and some do not allow them to work at all.

Children under school leaving age may do 'light work' (e.g. office work) provided that it does not interfere with their education or affect their health and safety. Certain types of work (e.g. factory work) are prohibited and any business employing children under school leaving age must obtain a permit from the local authority.

Subject to these points, children still attending school can work up to two hours most days. On Saturdays and weekdays during school holidays this is increased to eight hours (five hours if under 15). Working hours must fall between 7 am and 7 pm and are subject to an overall limit of 12 hours per week during term time or 35 hours during school holidays (25 hours if under 15). The child must also have at least two weeks of uninterrupted holiday each calendar year.

16 and 17 year olds over compulsory school age can generally work up to 40 hours per week and can do most types of work, although some additional health and safety regulations apply.

However, it should be noted that in England children must remain in some form of education or training until they reach 18 years old. This could be through part-time education or training whilst they are working; or through an apprenticeship.

Children aged 18 or more are mostly subject to the same employment rules as anyone else, including the working time directive.

In essence, therefore, you can generally employ any of your children aged 13 or more and pay them a salary which is deductible from your own business income.

How Much Can You Pay?

A salary paid to a child must be justified by the amount of work which they actually do in your business. If you employed your 15-year old daughter to answer your office phone one hour each evening, you could not justify paying her a salary of £30,000, but a salary of, say, £1,500 should be acceptable.

What about the national minimum wage? If your children are below the compulsory school leaving age the national minimum wage does not apply. The national minimum wage applies to employees aged 16 to 24 and the living wage applies to those aged 25 and over.

However, there is an exemption for relatives living in the employer's household. Hence, these compulsory wage rates will often not apply to your own children, although they may still be a good yardstick to use when setting the salary level for younger children with no particular business skills.

The hourly rates are as follows (with new rates applying from October 2016 in brackets):

- £7.20   Living wage, 25 and over
- £6.70 (£6.95) 21-24
- £5.30 (£5.55) 18-20
- £3.87 (£4.00) 16-17 if above school leaving age
- £3.30 (£3.40) apprentice rate

Subject to the national minimum wage (where it applies), there is no fixed rate of pay which applies to children. The rate paid must, however, be commercially justified – in other words, no more than you would pay to a non-family member with the same level of experience and ability in the job. For a child with no experience carrying out unskilled work, the national minimum wage for 16 to 17 year olds (currently £3.87 per hour) represents a good guide. Where the child has some experience, or the role requires some skill, a higher rate will often be justified.

Assuming that a rate of £5 per hour can be justified, the maximum salaries which a child could earn would be approximately as follows:

13/14 year olds:	£3,780
15+ but still school age:	£4,380
Over school age but under 18:	£10,400

Subject to this, a salary of up to £11,000 could be paid tax-free to a child aged under 16 with no other income.

For those aged 16 or more, any salary in excess of £8,060 will give rise to employee's National Insurance at 12% on the excess.

Employer's National Insurance at 13.8% generally applies to any payment in excess of £8,112 unless covered by the £3,000 employment allowance (see Chapter 7). However, there is an exemption for employees aged under 21 who are basic-rate taxpayers and an exemption for apprentices who are under 25 and basic-rate taxpayers.

Within the limits described above, every £100 of salary paid to a child by a higher rate tax-paying sole trader will save £42. Savings of up to £62 will be available in some cases.

Looked at another way, a higher rate taxpayer needs before tax income of £172.41 to be able to put £100 into a child's hands as pocket money. Alternatively, you can get them to do some work, pay them £100 and be left with £72.41 to spare (£42 after tax).

For a consideration of whether to pay salaries of more than £8,060 to children over school leaving age, take a look at Chapter 5: the issues are exactly the same.

Junior Partners

Taking one of your children into partnership may be a good way to reduce the overall tax burden on the family. This has important legal implications but using a Limited Liability Partnership ('LLP') is a good way to safeguard the family's private assets.

For children aged 21 and over, the position is much the same as taking a spouse into partnership and, once again, has the advantage of typically reducing the overall National Insurance burden from 25.8% to just 9% on profits between £8,060 and £43,000 allocated to the child (and from 15.8% to 2% on any excess) when compared with a salary.

In theory, there is nothing to prevent a minor child from being taken into partnership, even though they do not yet have full legal capacity to contract in their own right. Remember, however, that the National Insurance savings are much smaller for younger children because no employer's National Insurance is payable on salaries paid to under 21s who are basic-rate taxpayers.

The savings will also be much smaller if no employer's National Insurance is payable anyway thanks to the £3,000 employment allowance.

For a partnership to exist there must be an agreement for the partners to carry on in business together with a view to profit. This agreement may be express or implied and need not be written (except for an LLP), although this is generally advisable.

It must, however, be acted upon and it is here that HMRC will concentrate their attention and declare the partnership to be 'artificial' and thus null and void if this is not the case.

In other words, any child you take into partnership must genuinely participate in the business at a sufficient level to justify their status as a partner.

Trouble Ahead?

Under the right circumstances, partnership profits paid to both children and spouses are currently very tax efficient.

However, in 2007, the Government proposed to introduce new 'income shifting' legislation to tax any profits allocated to a child or spouse who was not active in the business as if they were the income of the parent or spouse who runs the business.

This legislation was postponed twice by the old Labour Government and is yet to re-emerge. Nevertheless, something like it may still come into force at some stage in the future.

To minimise any risk of adjustments under such new legislation, it is advisable to ensure that any child or spouse who is a partner is also actively involved in the business.

Conclusion

There are several different ways to save tax by effectively passing some of your business income directly to your children. It is vital to remember, however, that the income must be the child's to keep. Any arrangements requiring the child to pass the income back over to you will mean that the planning is ineffective and the income is taxed on you. You must truly give to truly save.

Part 3

Employing People

Chapter 7

The Hidden Cost:
Employer's National Insurance

When you employ somebody in your business, the wage or salary is a tax deductible expense.

Your employees will pay Income Tax and National Insurance but it is your responsibility, as HMRC's unofficial tax collector, to deduct it from their pay correctly and pay it over once a month.

You will also be required to report all payments made to employees to HMRC under the 'Real Time Information' system ('RTI'). Payments must be reported 'on or before' the point at which the payment is made.

These requirements will often lead to significant additional professional fees. Paying all your employees monthly (rather than weekly) will keep costs down, but they are often still a considerable burden for many businesses. Such costs are at least tax deductible, as you would expect.

Another much more significant cost is employer's National Insurance which can be much higher than the National Insurance paid by the employees themselves.

We call this the 'hidden cost' because many employees and budding entrepreneurs do not realise how much National Insurance is paid by employers!

There is, however, no employer's National Insurance on salaries paid to under 21s and apprentices under 25, provided, in both cases, salaries do not exceed £43,000.

Employees currently pay National Insurance at the following rates on their earnings:

- First £8,060   0%
- Next £34,940 12%
- Over £43,000 2%

Employers typically pay 13.8% on every pound that each employee earns in excess of £8,112, less the £3,000 employment allowance.

There is no cap on the employee's earnings for this purpose: the 13.8% rate continues to apply to any level of salary above £8,112.

Example
Eric employs five assistants (all aged 21 and over) and pays each of them £20,000 per year. He has to pay £6,310 in employer's National Insurance:

£20,000 - £8,112 = £11,888 x 13.8% = £1,641
x 5 =   £8,205
Less employer's allowance   £3,000
Equals   £5,205

This increases the cost of employing his assistants by over 5.2%.

Employer's National Insurance is Tax Deductible

Fortunately, employer's National Insurance is a tax deductible expense for the business. For self-employed business owners this means the employer's National Insurance that they pay will reduce their own tax bills.

Example continued
Eric is a higher-rate taxpayer. The £5,205 he pays in employer's National Insurance is a tax deductible expense and will reduce his own tax bill by £2,186 (£5,205 x 42%), so the true cost is only £3,019.

Chapter 8

Pay Your Employees Tax-Free Benefits

If you cannot afford to give your employees a pay rise one solution is to give them a variety of benefits-in-kind – if you cannot pay them more, pay them more tax efficiently!

To understand what sort of tax savings are available you have to remember that an employee's salary suffers three different taxes, two paid by the employee and one paid by the employer:

- Income Tax
- Employee's National Insurance
- Employer's National Insurance

With some benefits-in-kind ALL three taxes can be avoided, so there are significant savings to be had by both employees and employers.

Employer's National Insurance is the tax most employees forget about or don't even know about. It's levied at 13.8% on most salary income over £8,112. On a salary of £50,000 the employer will pay £5,781 in National Insurance – that's a lot of money that could have been kept by the employer or used to pay the employee a better salary.

When you add all three taxes together, the total Income Tax and National Insurance rates paid on salaries are currently as follows:

- Income from £8,060 to £11,000   25.8%
- Income from £11,000 to £43,000   45.8%
- Income from £43,000 to £100,000   55.8%
- Income from £100,000 to £122,000   75.8%
- Income from £122,000 to £150,000   55.8%
- Income over £150,000   60.8%

These combined tax rates are extremely ugly and I've never heard any politician mention them. They seem to live in a world where basic-rate taxpayers only pay 20% tax!

Premier League Benefits

Clearly any benefit in kind that avoids all of the three taxes is a much better alternative to cash salary.

The following are some of the benefits that are exempt from all three taxes:

- Workplace car parking
- Pension contributions
- One mobile phone
- Staff parties (costing up to £150 per head)
- Childcare vouchers
- Relocation costs (up to £8,000)
- Relevant training
- Provision of bicycles and cycling safety equipment
- Long-service awards
- In-house gyms and sports facilities
- Cheap/free canteen meals
- Gifts unconnected with work (e.g. wedding gifts)
- Business mileage payments
- Work and safety clothes
- Overnight expenses if away on business

Each of these tax-free benefits is subject to specific rules.

The Second Division

With many benefits-in-kind, the employee has to pay Income Tax at the usual rates (20%, 40% or 45%) and the employer has to pay National Insurance at 13.8% BUT there is no employee's National Insurance.

So most benefits-in-kind provide at least one tax saving: employee's National Insurance.

The employee's National Insurance saving doesn't amount to much if the employee is a higher-rate taxpayer. Higher-rate taxpayers only pay 2% National Insurance.

However, for basic-rate taxpayer employees, the saving is more substantial because they pay 12% National Insurance.

Example

Gaelene, a basic-rate taxpayer, pays £600 per year for her gym membership at Jim's Gym. Her employer, Trying to Please, offers to pay for her gym membership: Gaelene accepts.

Trying to Please contracts directly with Jim's Gym and pays the £600 annual cost. Adding 13.8% employer's National Insurance means the total cost to Trying to Please is £683. This amount is fully tax deductible, just like cash salary, so Trying to Please is not left out of pocket.

How much better off is Gaelene? She still faces an Income Tax charge of £120 but saves £72 of National Insurance (£600 x 12%).

Note that it is important that such an arrangement is structured correctly. If the gym membership is given in place of salary to which the employee has a contractual right, it will not work as planned.

It is also essential that the employer contracts directly with the gym. If the employer settles an employee's contractual liability, this will be fully taxable, like additional salary.

The tax saving is not large but it is an annual saving, so the same saving will be reaped in future years.

What is more, this is just one of many benefits-in-kind (e.g. medical insurance) that could be offered to Gaelene, so the total annual saving could be significant.

For the employer, the cost of providing a benefit is generally allowed as a tax-deductible expense because it is provided for the benefit of employees.

Further Savings - Discounts

If an employer has a significant number of employees, it may be possible to negotiate discounts with suppliers when contracting to provide employee benefits.

Example continued

Trying to Please offers gym membership to all of its 20 employees. The business obtains a 20% discount from Jim's Gym. The cost of a membership is normally £600. With the 20% bulk discount, the cost of an annual membership falls to £480.

So instead of paying a salary increase of £600 per employee, Trying to Please only has to pay gym memberships costing £480 per employee. Taking 13.8% National Insurance into account, the total saving is £137 per employee, or £2,740 for 20 employees.

Of course, the business may wish to structure things so that the employees share these savings, for example by offering gym membership plus a small pay increase.

VAT

With some benefits any input VAT paid by the employer is recoverable with no added output VAT charge. This is the case where the employer provides something that all employees may use for no deduction or reduction from their salary.

However, where there is a salary sacrifice or salary deduction, the business must pay output VAT. The taxable value of the benefit for VAT purposes will generally be the salary deducted or given up.

Time Cost

Although benefits-in-kind can provide attractive tax savings for the employer and the employee, the time cost should also be factored in. It would be much less time consuming for Trying to Please to just pay Gaelene some extra salary than set things up with Jim's Gym.

No one says being an employer is easy!

Chapter 9

Staff Entertaining Can Be Tax Free

The general rule is that entertainment expenditure is not tax deductible, e.g. entertaining business clients (see Chapter 13).

It comes as a surprise to many people that staff entertaining is, however, an allowable business expense.

The allowable costs of a staff function include food, drink, entertainment (e.g. musicians) and any other incidental costs, such as venue hire, transport and overnight accommodation.

VAT registered businesses can also recover VAT incurred on allowable staff entertaining expenditure.

There is no limit to the amount which a business can claim in respect of staff entertaining providing that there is no other motive behind the expenditure.

There are some restrictions to the scope of the relief, however, plus one major catch!

The first problem is that sole traders and business partners are proprietors, not staff, so entertaining spend for them *alone* is not allowable. So, you need to take some staff with you before any expenditure can be claimed.

Let's say that two business partners take their 12 office staff out for dinner to celebrate winning a new contract. That's fine: this expenditure would all be allowable and there is no need to restrict the claim for the element which relates to the proprietors themselves.

The motive behind the expenditure is important. Any staff entertaining undertaken to boost staff morale is an allowable cost as it is for the benefit of the business. Once there is any other relationship between proprietors and staff, however, the motive becomes less clear.

The most obvious example of this is where the staff member is also a relative: any entertaining expenditure in these cases is potentially a personal expense.

Nevertheless, where the relative is included in a larger group, the expenditure may remain allowable. A sole trader taking his four office staff to dinner could still claim all of the expenditure, even if his own son were one of them. If, however, he took the son out to dinner alone, the position would be very doubtful.

Even less clear is the position when a personal relationship develops between a proprietor and a member of staff. Again, we must look at the motive behind the expenditure. A close personal relationship would effectively put the staff member into the same category as a relative but what about a simple friendship?

In a small business, the proprietors and staff are all colleagues and friendships will often develop. This does not prevent you from claiming staff entertaining but the amount of expenditure claimed must be kept 'within reason'.

What is 'within reason' will depend on the circumstances of each case. A proprietor might take all the staff out for drinks every Friday evening. This is not unusual and the cost could be an allowable expense if motivating the staff appears to be the main reason for the expenditure. This, however, brings us to the catch!

The Catch

In principle, an employee is liable for Income Tax on the value of any benefit provided by reason of their employment. This includes the cost of staff entertaining. It even includes so-called benefits like the cost of sandwiches provided at a lunchtime staff meeting.

On top of this, the employer is also liable for Class 1A National Insurance at 13.8% on the cost of the staff entertaining. The 'cost' of entertaining, for both Income Tax and National Insurance purposes, must include VAT, even if the employer can recover it.

None of this affects the business's ability to claim a deduction for the expenditure. It's like a salary – the employee pays Income Tax, you pay employer's National Insurance and the business gets a tax deduction. (The only difference is that the employee does not also pay National Insurance, so there is a small saving.)

Nevertheless, taxing employees on entertaining spending is an absolute disaster when the original motive was improving staff morale. Any good done will be completely undone when the employees receive a tax bill. Can you imagine the countless arguments: "I only drank Water"; "I only went to show my face"; "I would never have gone if I knew I had to pay for it!"

Fortunately, there are a couple of ways to get around this problem. The employer could make a voluntary settlement. Better still, there's the annual party exemption.

The Annual Party Exemption

Expenditure of up to £150 per head on an annual staff function can be exempted from both Income Tax charges and employer's National Insurance. In fact, it doesn't have to be a single function and several events can be covered by the exemption, as long as the total aggregate cost per head over the tax year does not exceed £150.

This sounds great but there are a few pitfalls to watch out for:

- The exemption only covers annual events: either a Christmas party or a similar event. It does not cover 'casual hospitality', like taking the staff for a drink on a Friday night.

- The event must be open to all members of staff. It can be restricted to staff working at a particular location, such as a branch or regional office, but it cannot be restricted to staff of a particular grade, such as management only.

- Where the total cost of the event, including incidental costs like transport and overnight accommodation, and VAT (regardless of whether the business can recover it) exceeds £150 per head, none of the expenditure can be covered by the exemption. However, where there are several qualifying events in the year, the exemption can be used on any combination of these whose total aggregate cost adds up to no more than £150 per head.

Example

John, a sole trader, spends £160 per head on a Christmas party. None of this is covered by the exemption.

Jane, also a sole trader, spends £30 per head on a staff barbecue in May, £60 per head on a summer ball in August and £80 per head on a Christmas party. The exemption can be used to cover the summer ball and the Christmas party (total cost £140 per head), but the full cost of the staff barbecue will be taxable.

Quite bizarrely, Jane has spent £10 more per head on staff entertaining but her staff are taxable on a cost of only £30 each compared with £160 for John's staff.

As we can see, careful planning of the timing and scale of your staff functions will enable you to make the most of the exemption.

The good news is that the cost per head is calculated by dividing the total cost of the event by the number of people attending, including staff's partners and other guests. Sometimes this could mean that increasing the size of the event reduces the cost per head to the point where the exemption applies.

One way to keep the cost of an event to no more than £150 per head is to advise staff that they will be required to reimburse any costs in excess of this amount. However, this may not be good for morale and a fixed contribution in advance of the event is usually more acceptable to staff.

Staff Entertaining versus Business Entertaining

Where customers or other external parties are present at an event, it may become business entertaining rather than staff entertaining. The business is unable to claim a tax deduction but there is no tax charge on staff attending the event, nor any Class 1A National Insurance.

Given the cost of a voluntary settlement, this may actually work out cheaper.

Voluntary Settlements

For expenditure not covered by the annual party exemption, there is another way to prevent morale-shattering tax charges from falling on the staff, but it comes at a cost.

The employer can negotiate a voluntary settlement with HMRC and pay all the Income Tax and National Insurance arising. This payment is treated much like PAYE, so the payment itself is usually tax deductible.

To arrange a voluntary settlement, it is sensible for you to approach HMRC first and to provide full details of all the staff entertaining costs which you wish to cover under the settlement. You may also wish to include other items, such as sandwiches provided at lunchtime meetings or pizzas bought for staff working late (oh yes, these are a taxable benefit). The deadline for making a voluntary settlement is 6th July following the tax year involved.

You will then need to agree a suitable rate to gross up the cost to allow for the fact that you are settling the staff's Income Tax liability. Finally, you will need to add on Class 1A National Insurance.

Example

Omar, a sole trader, spends a total of £3,000 on a staff party (including VAT) which is not covered by the annual party exemption. He advises HMRC that he wishes to make a voluntary settlement rather than allow his staff to be taxed on this benefit.

Half of the staff at the party were basic rate taxpayers, so the grossed up cost of their benefit is £1,500 x 100/80 = £1,875. The other half were higher rate taxpayers, producing a grossed up cost of £1,500 x 100/60 = £2,500. The total grossed up cost is thus £4,375, giving rise to a tax charge of £1,375 (£4,375 - £3,000) plus Class 1A National Insurance of £604 (£4,375 x 13.8%).

Omar's voluntary settlement is £1,979 (£1,375 + £604). This is 66% of the cost of the party, but at least Omar can claim it as a tax deduction in his own accounts.

Chapter 10

Auto-Enrolment: The Advent of Compulsory Pensions

A new system of compulsory pensions known as 'auto enrolment' is forcing employers to enrol nearly all their staff into a pension between October 2012 and February 2018.

Whether you view this as a good or bad thing probably depends on your political leanings... and whether you are an employer or employee.

When it comes to pensions, many small business owners cannot afford to save for their own retirements, let alone those of their entire workforce... they have a tough enough job already paying PAYE, National Insurance, VAT, Business Rates etc, etc, ... as well as their own tax bill on what little income they have left!

To find out what date applies to your business, use the timeline tool available at:

www.thepensionsregulator.gov.uk/employers/staging-date.aspx

Exemptions

Employees exempt from auto enrolment include those:

- Earning below the 'earnings trigger' (£10,000 in 2016/17)
- Under 22 years of age
- Over state pension age
- Company directors not considered to be 'employed' or the only worker in the business
- Already in a qualifying pension scheme

Certain groups of employees do not need to be auto-enrolled but must be given the right to opt in if they want, including those:

- Over 16 and under 22
- Over state pension age and under 75
- With earnings between the lower earnings limit and the earnings trigger (£5,824-£10,000 for 2016/17)

How Much Will it Cost?

Employers are forced to make a minimum pension contribution and, in practice, so too are most employees.

Generally speaking, contributions are a percentage of 'qualifying earnings'. The minimum contribution will be increased gradually until April 2019.

Contributions start at 2% with at least 1% coming from the employer. From 6 April 2019 onwards the total minimum contribution will be 8%, with at least 3% coming from the employer.

The minimum contributions are as follows:

	Employer pays	Total required	Employee could pay
Employer's staging date to 5 April 2018	1%	2%	1%
6 April 2018 to 5 April 2019	2%	5%	3%
From 6 April 2019	3%	8%	5%

The total minimum contribution can be paid by the employer but in practice many small firms will probably insist that the employee makes up the required balance.

This means that from 6 April 2019 onwards many employees will be forced to contribute 5% to a pension if they want to benefit from a 3% contribution from their employer.

Employees' contributions will enjoy tax relief as normal, which means 4% will come from them personally and the extra 1% will be added by the taxman in the form of basic-rate tax relief.

Qualifying Earnings

The minimum contributions are generally not based on the employee's total earnings but rather on a band of earnings.

The lower and upper thresholds for 2016/17 are £5,824 and £43,000 respectively. What this means is that pension contributions are typically based on earnings of up to £37,176 (£43,000 - £5,824).

For example, someone with employment income of £50,000 will have their pension contributions based on earnings of £37,176. Someone with employment income of £20,000 will have their pension contributions based on earnings of £14,176 (£20,000 - £5,824).

Pension Schemes

A state-sponsored pension scheme called NEST (National Employment Savings Trust) is available for employers who do not have their own pension scheme. You can use another scheme if you prefer but it must be a "qualifying scheme". The pension provider will be able to tell you if the scheme is qualifying or not.

Employees Can Opt Out

Employees will be automatically enrolled but employers can postpone this by up to three months. The three month period is designed to make life easier for businesses that employ lots of temporary and seasonal workers.

It is important to note that employees can opt out of compulsory pensions if they choose.

Some employees may choose to opt out because it's not just their employers who are going to be forced to make pension contributions. Employees will also have to put money in and their contributions will be even higher than their employer's (5% from April 2019, albeit with 1% coming from the taxman).

Many employees may choose to spend their earnings rather than save for the future, especially those in their twenties, thirties and forties, faced with paying off student loans, climbing the housing ladder and bringing up children.

In short, the easiest way for employers to avoid compulsory pension contributions may simply be to inform their employees that they can opt out if they want to. Care must be taken, however, as employers are prohibited from inducing or encouraging employees to opt out. Any decision to opt out must be taken freely by the staff member without influence from the employer.

If the employee does, however, opt out the employer doesn't have to make any contributions.

Part 4

Business Travel, Subsistence and Entertainment

Chapter 11

Travel Expenses: How to Claim a Bigger Deduction

Travel takes many forms: trains, taxis, planes, cars; the list is almost endless. In most cases, the cost is obvious, such as a train ticket or taxi fare.

Motor expenses are a little harder to calculate and we will look at these in more detail in Part 7. Here, however, we focus on the issue of what constitutes business travel.

Whatever method we travel by, the cost is an allowable expense for tax purposes if the journey is classed as a **business journey**.

You would think this would be a simple matter. Straight away though, we run into a problem.

Principle 1: Home to work travel is not allowable

Imagine a self-employed woman called Jo, travelling to her business premises every day. To a reasonable layman, this journey is clearly made for business purposes. Sadly, tax law states otherwise and this journey is classed as personal.

Principle 2: Travel from home to a temporary workplace is allowable

What if Jo needs to carry out some work at her customer's premises and travels there directly from home? Now the journey is classed as a business journey.

In general, travel to a workplace remains allowable unless that workplace is intended to be the individual's permanent base, or actually becomes their work base for a period of two years or more. Jo cannot claim the cost of travel from her home to her office but can claim the cost of travel from her home to any other business destination, unless it becomes her main base for two years or more.

People working from home can therefore generally claim all of their business travel costs since there is no 'home to work' element to be disallowed.

Principle 3: Where there is 'Triangular Travel' involving home, work and another business destination, two sides of the triangle will be allowable (but not the 'home to work' side)

If Jo leaves her customer's premises and goes straight home, this journey is again allowable. Alternatively, if Jo travels from the customer to her office, this journey is also allowable.

Let us suppose that Jo lives in Bedford and works in Luton. A journey from her home to a customer in Milton Keynes would be fully allowable and the subsequent journey from Milton Keynes either to Luton or back to Bedford would also be fully allowable. However, if Jo goes to her office in Luton after visiting the customer, her later journey back home to Bedford will not then be allowable.

Principle 4: Any part of a journey which is part of, or similar to, a person's usual home to work journey is not allowable

HM Revenue & Customs (HMRC) views journeys which are similar to a person's regular commute as still being 'home to work travel'.

Where there is a clearly separate additional business element to a journey, however, that element should remain allowable.

Let's say Jo visits another customer based a few miles from her office. She catches the train to Luton as usual but, instead of walking to her office nearby, she takes taxis to her customer and back to her office afterwards. Jo's taxi journeys are allowable since they are clearly not part of her usual journey to work.

Principle 5: There is no restriction on the standard, or class, of travel for the purposes of tax relief

Jo visits London on business and travels first class. Despite the increased cost, the journey remains fully allowable.

In fact, Jo could travel to Istanbul first class by Orient Express if she wished and there would be no restriction on her tax relief as long as the journey was made purely for business purposes. If she stopped off in Venice for some sightseeing, however, the journey would cease to be wholly for business purposes and would not be fully allowable.

Principle 6: Small incidental private elements to a journey will not prevent it from being allowable

In theory, the cost of travel is only allowable when incurred 'wholly and exclusively' for business purposes. Taking this literally would mean that any personal element to a journey would prevent the entire cost from being allowed for tax purposes.

Thankfully, HMRC is prepared to ignore any minor, incidental element to a journey. If Jo stopped at a garage to buy some milk on her way home from a customer, for example, the journey would remain fully allowable.

This leaves us with the problem of journeys with a more significant private element to them.

Principle 7: The main reason behind a journey will usually determine whether it is allowable

Grant is another customer whom Jo often visits. However, Grant is also a personal friend and Jo will often stay for dinner afterwards.

Here, we have to ask what the main purpose of the journey was. If Jo's main reason for visiting Grant was for business and staying for dinner was merely incidental, then the journey remains fully allowable. On the other hand, if she mainly went to Grant's for dinner and they just happened to discuss a little business then the journey is a private one and not allowable at all.

Principle 8: Where there is more than one purpose to the journey, an apportionment will usually be accepted

So what about that trip on the Orient Express? Theory says that the journey is not 'wholly and exclusively' for business purposes and therefore not allowable.

In practice, however, for self-employed taxpayers, HMRC will usually accept a reasonable apportionment between the business and private elements. Some claim might therefore still be justified, although the exact proportion will depend on the facts of the case and any additional costs relating directly to Jo's stay in Venice would have to be disallowed.

We will return to the subject of international travel in more detail in Chapter 14.

Chapter 12

Subsistence:
How to Claim a Bigger Deduction

Almost every business owner incurs subsistence expenditure such as meals, drinks and other refreshments, yet in practice it can often be one of the most difficult areas of tax to deal with.

Business Proprietors

The greatest area of difficulty tends to arise with business proprietors' own subsistence costs – the expenses incurred directly by sole traders, business partners and individuals with property rental businesses.

Claims for proprietors' own subsistence must usually be based on actual expenditure and 'round sum' allowances are not generally available.

The first problem is evidence. Many business owners neglect to obtain receipts for some of their subsistence expenditure.

Here, I would make two points:

- Firstly, in an ideal world, you should really try to get a receipt for every last penny of your business subsistence. It doesn't necessarily have to be a printed till receipt: I have even resorted to getting a receipt written on a napkin!

- Secondly, don't just give up and not make a claim just because you don't have a receipt. Reasonable subsistence claims are seldom refused, especially if you make a note of the expenditure at the time – but do try to get receipts in future.

Business Trips

The basic rule is that business proprietors may claim reasonable subsistence costs incurred during a business trip.

In essence, a business trip is any trip away from the proprietor's normal place of business made for business purposes and which does not form part of their normal pattern of travel (see Chapter 11).

Let's look at a couple of examples to see what this means in practice.

Example 1
Mike is based in Scotland and has to spend a day in London on business. He has an early morning flight, so he has breakfast at the airport. He grabs a coffee and a Danish pastry when he arrives in London. Later, he goes out for lunch in a pub near his customer's office. He buys another coffee and a piece of cake in the airport on the way home.

All of this expenditure was necessitated by Mike's business trip and can all be claimed for tax purposes.

If, however, Mike buys himself a takeaway on the way home from the airport that evening, it would not be allowable. If he had dinner in London before catching his flight home though, this would be allowable.

An interesting planning point emerges here. By and large, any meals, snacks or drinks you have while you're away will be allowable. As soon as you're back on your own 'patch', any further expenditure is purely personal and cannot be claimed.

Example 2
Emma normally works from home but needs to visit one of her customers just a mile away. She buys herself a coffee on the way to her customer's office and goes for lunch in a local cafe.

Sadly, this expenditure is not allowable. Emma could have made herself a coffee before leaving home and could have returned home for lunch. Her subsistence expenditure cannot be claimed as a business expense because she had a reasonable alternative.

It would have been exactly the same if Emma had her own office premises and her customer's office was only a mile away from there. Her subsistence costs would still have been a personal expense because one cannot say that her expenditure was any different to that which she might incur during a normal day at her own office.

Mike, on the other hand, flew all the way to London. It would have been ridiculous to expect him to go home to Scotland for lunch, so his subsistence costs were a reasonable business expense.

There is no set rule on how far you must travel before your subsistence costs become allowable. It is a question of whether it would have been reasonable for you to return home, or to the area in which your own business premises are located, before incurring the expense.

You must also actually incur the expenditure during the business trip. In Mike's case, it would be quite reasonable for him to have dinner in London, which would be allowable, but if he chose to go home first, he could not claim the cost of his dinner in Scotland.

Whilst subsistence expenditure needs to be reasonable, it doesn't need to be frugal. If you're in a town with a nice Italian restaurant and a burger bar, there is no requirement for you to take the cheaper option.

Alcohol

Some people assume that all alcohol must be a personal expense and hence not allowable. Not so! Just because something provides an element of personal enjoyment, this does not prevent it from being a business expense. You wouldn't just assume that desserts weren't allowable, would you?

You have to drink, so if you choose to drink one or two glasses of beer or wine with a meal instead of water or lemonade, it's still subsistence expenditure. A single glass of beer or wine in an airport or railway station on your way home would also generally be allowable.

But, any expense you claim must be reasonable. There can come a point when the expense is incurred purely for personal enjoyment and is no longer allowable. A half bottle of wine is usually fine, but a magnum of vintage champagne is probably not.

Similarly, whilst drinks taken with a meal are usually considered reasonable, further alcoholic drinks after an evening meal would generally be regarded as a personal cost which cannot be claimed.

Business Meetings and Entertaining

So far, we've talked about personal subsistence. Once you're with a customer or business contact, the situation changes.

For business meetings, we must again consider what is reasonable. A cup of tea or coffee whilst you discuss some business would usually be acceptable. Beyond that, we're into the realm of business entertaining and that's another story (see Chapter 13).

In the meantime, if you're reading this in an airport or railway station on your way home from a business trip, why not have a drink on the Chancellor of the Exchequer?

Chapter 13

Entertainment Can Be Tax Deductible

Back in the early 1980s, the cost of entertaining foreign customers was an allowable expense for tax purposes. Sadly, however, despite being a vital and unavoidable expense for many businesses, there is no longer any tax deduction available for any business entertaining, foreign and domestic alike.

At first glance, therefore, there might seem to be little point in writing a chapter on business entertaining. In my experience, however, a great deal of allowable expenditure is wrongly classed as business entertaining and disallowed when it could legitimately be claimed as something else.

Furthermore, with a few minor changes in business behaviour, even more expenditure might be deductible.

Subsistence

The first area of confusion is the difference between subsistence and entertaining. If you take a customer to lunch, the cost of their meal is business entertaining and not deductible. If you took them to lunch locally, the cost of your own meal must be treated the same way.

If you have travelled some distance to meet the customer, however, your own meal might represent a legitimate subsistence cost which may be claimed (see Chapter 12).

This is why it is generally a mistake to 'play host' to your visitors. A policy of 'visitor pays' could convert half of your entertaining expenditure into allowable subsistence costs.

Example
Every month, Mike travels 100 miles to visit Linda, one of his suppliers. Linda pays for their lunch in a local restaurant. Linda also visits Mike

once a month and he then pays for lunch. All of the costs incurred by both Mike and Linda are disallowable business entertaining.

Let us suppose, however, that Mike and Linda reverse their arrangements to a 'visitor pays' policy. Half of the cost of each lunch now becomes allowable subsistence expenditure.

The position changes if a visitor is actually making a direct contribution to your business – i.e. they are personally performing work directly for your business during their visit.

Let us suppose that Linda is an IT consultant and, during her visits, she carries out maintenance work on Mike's computer system. If Mike pays for Linda's lunch under these circumstances, he can claim this as part of his IT support costs.

Furthermore, where there is a contractual obligation to provide visitors with food, drink, etc, this cost is also usually allowable.

Staff Entertaining

Staff entertaining is an exception to the normal rules on entertaining and is generally an allowable expense for tax purposes, although it can lead to additional PAYE costs (see Chapter 9 for details). However, this exception does not apply if the staff entertaining is merely incidental to the entertainment of customers or other non-employee guests.

The test that HM Revenue and Customs uses to assess this is to consider whether the employer would still have paid for the event if the non-employee guests had not been present. If the employer would not have paid without the presence of other guests, the staff entertaining is merely incidental and none of the cost is allowable.

Hence, for example, inviting a member of staff to join you and a customer for lunch will not turn the cost of the meal into allowable staff entertaining – it will remain non-deductible business entertaining (there would be no PAYE charges though).

Alternatively, you might have already arranged to take some staff out for lunch when a visitor arrives unexpectedly. So, you ask them to join you for lunch – now you only need to disallow the cost of the visitor's meal.

Better still, why not invite some customers to your annual staff party? You would still need to disallow an appropriate proportion of the cost, but this will often be more cost effective than having to disallow the cost of separately entertaining each customer.

Look at it this way: you and two business partners have a party and invite twelve staff and five customers. You will need to disallow a quarter of the cost (5 out of 20). If you had taken each customer to lunch separately, the whole cost of all five lunches would have been disallowable.

Travel and Incidental Costs

Incidental costs related to business entertaining, such as travel expenses, must generally also be disallowed. This would apply, for example, where you invited a customer to dinner and paid their taxi fare. The travel costs for employees attending their employer's own business entertaining event are allowable, however.

As for sole traders and business partners' own travel expenses when attending a business entertaining event, the position is not totally clear. However, such costs should be allowable where an event also includes a business element, such as where a business meeting is followed by dinner afterwards. In fact, where an event does have such a mixed purpose, the travel costs of all attendees should be allowable.

Inclusive Costs

In many businesses, it is customary to provide customers with basic hospitality, such as tea or coffee and perhaps a few biscuits. This is effectively basic office etiquette and may also apply in other situations, such as hairdressers' salons, for example.

Where such basic hospitality can be regarded as a normal part of the service being provided, the cost should be allowable.

Meals, accommodation and other entertaining expenses may also sometimes be included as part of a 'package' of services provided to customers. If so, the cost of these items is allowable. This might apply, for example, where a business sells residential training courses which include meals and accommodation.

Promotional Events

In principle, the cost of a promotional event arranged to publicise your business or its products is allowable. This includes the cost of any of your own products or services provided free as part of the event. However, the cost of any food, drink or other hospitality provided as part of the event is usually disallowable.

For example, a car dealer could have a 'track day' at which potential customers could drive its cars on a racetrack. The cost of renting the track, providing the cars and the no doubt astronomical insurance for the event would all be allowable, but the cost of any food or drink provided would be disallowable.

If, however, the dealer charged for the event as a commercial venture in its own right (i.e. not subsidised), or provided the event to actual customers only on a contractual basis as part of their purchase, then the whole cost of the entire event would be fully allowable.

Employees' Entertaining Expenses

Where an employer makes a direct reimbursement of business entertaining expenses incurred by employees, the cost is disallowable in the usual way. However, where an employee is paid a general expense allowance to cover all expenditure, this will remain fully allowable (although, once again, this may have PAYE consequences and may not always be beneficial overall).

Chapter 14

Travel Abroad and Claim the Cost

How do you get the taxman to pay for part of the cost of trips abroad?

At one end of the spectrum there is the pure business trip. You may need to travel to some far-flung location to meet customers, suppliers or business colleagues, or to view sites for some new venture abroad.

Just because your trip takes you far away doesn't prevent it from being a business trip and the travel, subsistence and accommodation costs involved remain fully allowable for tax purposes under the general principles which we have explored in the previous chapters.

Many business trips will, however, have some 'leisure' element to them. Your foreign host might take you to dinner, for example. Such minor, incidental, personal elements to the trip should not make any difference and the whole cost of the trip should still be allowable.

It would be slightly different if you paid for that dinner yourself though. Your own meal would represent allowable subsistence expenditure, but the cost of anyone else's meal (other than an employee of your own business) would usually represent entertaining expenditure and hence not be allowed as a tax deduction.

For longer trips abroad, the 'leisure' element of the trip often becomes more significant. At this point, we have to start separating out the business and private elements of the trip in order to establish how much is allowable. A lot will depend on the circumstances surrounding the trip. The most important factor in many cases will be your initial rationale for taking the trip in the first place.

Example

James is self-employed and has his own import-export business. He needs to visit Hi Fat, one of his suppliers, in Bangkok. Hi Fat organises a meeting on Monday, a factory tour on Tuesday and another meeting on Wednesday.

There are no available flights arriving in Bangkok on Sunday, so James has to travel on Saturday, leaving him a free day on the Sunday. James spends the day sightseeing and goes to a Thai boxing match in the evening. He spends £100 on entry fees (for museums, etc, and the boxing match) and £60 on food and drink during the day. His accommodation also costs £200 per night.

Although James has spent the day sightseeing, he is in Bangkok purely for business reasons, so he is able to claim the cost of his food and drink and his accommodation on Saturday and Sunday nights.

The cost of James's flights also remains fully allowable, as his sole purpose for taking the trip was to meet Hi Fat.

The only costs which James cannot claim in these circumstances are his £100 of entry fees.

So, simply occupying your free time abroad in a pleasurable way still leaves you able to claim the vast majority of the cost of your trip.

So far, I'm assuming that James flew back home as soon as possible after concluding his business with Hi Fat, but what if he extended his trip?

Extending Your Trip

By Wednesday night, James's business in Bangkok is finished. However, he does not fly home until Saturday morning and spends all of Thursday and Friday sightseeing.

The position now will depend on the reason behind James's decision to not book a flight home until Saturday.

If Saturday was the earliest available return flight, or the cost of any earlier flight was significantly greater, then the extension to James's trip was purely business-driven. He would then be able to continue to claim all subsistence and accommodation costs in full, as well as the cost of his flights.

'Subsistence', for this purpose, would generally include all non-alcoholic drinks at any time and any alcoholic drinks taken with meals. James would have to disallow any purely personal costs incurred, such as entry fees to museums, shows, etc.

If, however, James could have flown home on Thursday, but decided to extend his trip for personal reasons, then the situation is quite different. Here there are several potential scenarios to consider.

Firstly, let's suppose that James genuinely needed to visit Hi Fat for bona fide business reasons and then subsequently decided that, as he was going all the way to Bangkok, he might as well extend his trip to give him a chance to see the city.

The primary purpose for James's trip is therefore still business and he can continue to claim full relief for the cost of his flights and all his subsistence and accommodation costs from his arrival on the first Saturday until Wednesday night, plus any subsistence costs during his journey home.

In other words, James will only need to disallow the additional costs incurred due to extending his trip by an extra two days (as well as all purely personal costs such as entry fees for shows, etc).

James will have spent seven nights in Bangkok so a simple way to look at his accommodation costs would be to disallow two sevenths of the total bill (his first night's accommodation remains allowable as he had no choice but to fly in a day early).

However, he only needs to disallow the additional costs of extending his trip, so it may sometimes be worth 'digging a little deeper'. Suppose, for example, that it would have cost £1,000 to stay for five nights but that the hotel only charges £1,300 for seven nights. James's disallowable accommodation cost would then be just £300.

James could also improve his position by planning his dining habits carefully. Meal costs incurred up to Wednesday night (the business part of his trip) will be allowable but his meals on Thursday and Friday are a personal expense. Hence, if there are any more expensive restaurants which James would like to try out, he should do so by Wednesday night!

Mixed Purpose for Trip

In our second scenario, let's suppose that James's reasons for travelling to Bangkok were mixed. Visiting Hi Fat was useful, but not essential, and James also fancied a few days' break in Thailand.

Now we have to take a completely different approach to apportioning James's expenditure. We start by separating out any elements which are purely business (like a taxi fare from James's hotel to Hi Fat's office) or purely personal (like James's entry fee to the Thai boxing match).

Subsistence costs should be allocated according to whether they were incurred during a 'business day' (Monday to Wednesday) or a 'leisure day' (Sunday, Thursday and Friday).

The remaining costs, including flights, accommodation and subsistence costs on James's 'travel days' (both Saturdays), have a 'mixed' purpose. A self-employed person like James could then claim a reasonable proportion of these costs. In this particular case, James had six full days in Bangkok and spent three of these on business, so he could reasonably claim three sixths, or 50%.

For a self-employed person, the costs allowed for a 'mixed' trip like this are not too dissimilar to an extended business trip like our first scenario. James does, however, lose the ability to claim full relief for the cost of his flights and his allowable accommodation costs would reduce from £1,000 to £650 (£1,300 x 50%). He is also unable to claim subsistence costs on Sunday, as he can no longer argue that he was only in Bangkok for business reasons.

Lastly, let's suppose that James had actually already booked a holiday in Bangkok and then decided to visit Hi Fat while he was there. This is pretty much the 'mirror image' of our first scenario. The primary purpose of the trip is personal, so it is only the additional costs incurred in visiting Hi Fat which can be claimed.

This means that James would not be able to claim any relief for his flights or his accommodation. All that he could claim would be additional travel costs (e.g. taxi fares) and subsistence incurred whilst visiting Hi Fat. This may sound ridiculously unfair, but remember that James is basically on holiday. You can't turn a holiday into a business trip just by popping in on a business acquaintance while you're there!

To avoid this fate, you should arrange the business part of your trip first before you book your flights or accommodation.

Internal Travel

The treatment of internal travel costs, such as taxi or train fares, incurred whilst abroad on business, depends on the reason for the internal trip. A purely business journey will be fully allowable and a journey made for personal reasons, such as sightseeing or going to a show, will be fully disallowable. Travel costs incurred when going out for meals may be allowable, depending on the circumstances. For a self-employed person on a purely business trip, or a 'business day' during a 'mixed' trip, these will be allowable.

Business Conferences

For many people, their main experience of foreign business travel is the business conference. In theory, the principles for claiming tax relief for the costs of attending a conference are exactly the same as for other business trips. In practice, however, conferences do seem to give rise to a few problems!

A typical business conference will involve some lectures or presentations, meals, refreshments, accommodation and some business networking activities. It's that last category that causes the problems because 'networking' often involves some form of leisure activities.

For example, a conference in Florida might include an afternoon's golf. Is it still a business trip? If the golf is an integral part of the conference and the only people involved are conference delegates and organisers, I would argue that this is a pure business networking activity and the entire cost of attending the conference remains allowable. HM Revenue and Customs have been known to disagree with this view in similar situations however.

Chapter 15

Travelling Abroad with a Spouse or Partner

In the previous chapter we looked at foreign travel costs and how much of them can be claimed for tax purposes. In this chapter we will take a look at the tax position for trips taken together with a spouse, partner, or other family member.

For ease of illustration, I'm actually just going to talk about being accompanied by your spouse. As far as the tax treatment is concerned, however, being accompanied by an unmarried life partner or any other member of your family has much the same effect.

The Nature of the Trip

The first thing to consider is: what is the main reason for taking the trip?

Is your spouse accompanying you on a business trip, or are you simply fitting some business into a holiday or other private trip?

In the former case, you are likely to be able to claim a significant proportion of the cost of the trip, in the latter you will generally only be able to claim any additional costs arising as a direct result of the business element of the trip.

The mere fact that your spouse accompanies you on a trip does initially tend to suggest that there is at least some private element. This can be overcome in some cases, but it is necessary to show that your spouse's presence was required for business purposes.

Working Spouses

In some cases, your spouse will actually work in your business, perhaps as a fellow partner, or employed as your personal assistant, or in some other capacity. Whatever their role, there could be a genuine business reason for them to accompany you on the trip. This makes it a business trip for each of you and a suitable proportion of the travel, accommodation and subsistence costs for both of you can be claimed following the same principles as we looked at in Chapter 14.

Note, however, that this generally only covers situations where your spouse has a permanent role in your business which is consistent with the need to take them on the business trip with you. Hiring your spouse as a clerical assistant for a couple of weeks while you're abroad will not usually be enough!

Social and Networking Requirements

Sometimes you might need to take your spouse on a business trip in order to meet the cultural or social expectations of a foreign host or business contact.

Let us suppose, for example, that, in order to secure a large contract in South America, the Managing Director of a UK company flies to Rio for some business meetings and is also invited to dinner at his opposite number's home. The South American host clearly expects the UK director to take his wife with him and, although this is ostensibly a social occasion, the contract rides on meeting those expectations.

In this situation, the travel costs in respect of the UK director's wife are wholly, exclusively and necessarily incurred for business purposes and are therefore fully allowable.

However, it does not take much of a change to this situation before the spouse's travel costs cease to be allowable. If it is merely desirable, rather than essential, for the MD's wife to accompany the MD to the dinner in Rio then her travel costs become a personal expense. The company could still get relief for those costs but the MD would then be personally liable for a benefit in kind charge on them, giving rise to combined Income Tax and National Insurance costs of up to 58.8% (45% Income Tax for the MD and 13.8% National Insurance for the company).

The position is a little better for sole traders and business partners. Where their spouse accompanies them on a business trip, the spouse's presence on the trip only needs to be 'wholly and exclusively for business purposes' in order for the costs to be allowable.

"What's the difference?" you may ask! The difference is that, as an employee, the MD can only classify his wife's travel costs as a business expense when it is essential that she accompanies him on the trip whereas a sole trader or business partner can claim their spouse's travel costs when the spouse's presence is merely desirable.

What I mean here is that the spouse's presence must be desirable for business purposes, such as to impress that South American business contact. Furthermore, this must be the main or only reason for the spouse going on the trip.

The great difficulty in many cases is in establishing exactly what the main reason for the spouse to go on the trip is. Imagine you take your spouse to Rio for three days so that they can accompany you to that business dinner and help you win that contract. The dinner takes up one evening, leaving your spouse with two and a half days of free time while you attend other business meetings, etc.

If your spouse stayed in your hotel room for two and a half days and only emerged to go to the business dinner then it would be easy to demonstrate that they had come to Rio purely for business reasons. But that would be ridiculous. Whatever the initial reason was for the trip, most people are going to make the most of any free time they have. This should not change the underlying nature of the trip although, of course, any additional expenses incurred in sightseeing, going to shows, visiting friends and relatives, etc, will all be disallowable private expenses.

The problem is that the fact that your spouse will naturally want to occupy their free time in a pleasurable way will make it very difficult to establish that there was a clear business motive for taking them on the trip in the first place. Any documentation recording the rationale for your spouse's presence on the trip will be helpful: especially in the case of a partnership where the other partners' approval might be required. It would also be wise to ensure that all of the business elements of the trip are arranged first before adding on any private elements like a visit to the theatre or a boat trip.

Where there is a mixture of business and private reasons for a sole trader or business partner to take their spouse with them, it may be possible to claim part of the spouse's travel costs in a similar way to the costs of the mixed purpose trips which we looked at in Chapter 14. The stronger the business case for taking your spouse, the greater the proportion of the costs you are likely to be able to claim.

Purely Private Spouses

Where the business owner has simply taken their spouse with them on a business trip for purely personal reasons, the owner's own travel costs will be allowable on the same basis as we looked at in Chapter 14, but the spouse's costs will be a personal expense.

It would, however, only be necessary to disallow any additional costs incurred as a result of the spouse's presence on the trip. For example, there may not be any additional accommodation costs to disallow, as the room charge might have been the same whether the spouse was there or not. The same might apply to taxi fares or the costs of hiring a car.

That Special Person

If the spouse has some special skill which is relevant to the business owner's trip then the cost of taking them along might then become allowable. A good example might be a spouse who speaks the local language and can therefore act as an interpreter.

The spouse's expenses might also be allowable where the business owner is in such poor health that they must accompany them.

Finally, a business owner might claim the cost of taking their spouse where this was essential to their personal safety. This would be particularly relevant in the case of a female business owner travelling to a developing country but might also apply to a businessman whose wife has a black belt in karate!

Part 5

Investing in Your Business:
Capital Allowances

Chapter 16

Capital Allowances: The Basics

When your business spends money on most things like rent, wages, or stationery, the cost is instantly tax deductible in full.

In other words, if you spend £10,000 on rent during the year, your taxable profits will be reduced by £10,000 and your tax bill will fall by £4,200 if you are a higher-rate taxpayer (£10,000 x 42%).

However, when your business buys *assets* – things that are not used up during the year but last for several years – you may not be able to claim a full tax deduction in the year of purchase. Instead, you may only be able to claim, say, 18% per year.

This 18% tax deduction is known as a capital allowance and is designed to compensate your business for asset depreciation due to wear and tear.

Capital allowances are given instead of commercial depreciation charges included in your accounts, which are not allowable.

What Sort of Spending Gets Capital Allowances?

Generally speaking it is spending on 'plant and machinery' that qualifies for capital allowances. Plant and machinery is a somewhat old-fashioned term and there is no definition of it in the statute books.

For a typical business in the service sector, plant and machinery includes things like:

- Computers and office equipment
- Office furniture
- Cars and other vehicles

Businesses that 'make things', for example those in the manufacturing sector or construction sector, usually own specialist equipment and tools.

These assets also attract capital allowances, although there are far too many to mention.

Spending that Does Not Qualify

Almost every asset you buy for your business will attract capital allowances. There are very few exceptions, the most notable ones being:

- Stock-in-trade
- Buildings and land

Stock in trade is simply the inventory or merchandise belonging to the business: the stuff it sells! Not all businesses sell goods but, for those that do, the tax treatment is covered in Chapter 38.

Buildings and land also do not qualify for capital allowances because these assets tend to rise in value over time, rather than depreciate.

Although buildings and land do not qualify for capital allowances, certain 'integral features' inside commercial properties do qualify.

Integral features include all the existing wiring, lighting, plumbing, heating and air conditioning in any commercial property you buy for your business. (Chapter 32 takes a detailed look at spending on integral features.)

Tax relief is also available when you spend money on certain property fixtures, including new fitted bathrooms, toilets, showers, and kitchens in any commercial property.

This is as close as you can get to claiming tax relief for the building itself.

Annual Investment Allowance

UK tax legislation contains a generous 'annual investment allowance', which provides 100% tax relief for spending on most types of plant and machinery.

The allowance is available for purchases of both new and second-hand assets and is available to all types of business: sole traders, partnerships and companies alike.

The allowance was increased to £500,000 in 2014 and was due to fall back to £25,000 in January 2016. However, with effect from 1st January 2016, it has now been fixed permanently at £200,000.

Transitional Rules

Transitional rules apply to accounting periods which straddle the date of the change on 1st January 2016. The maximum annual investment allowance for the whole period is calculated on a pro rata basis.

For example, in the case of a sole trader with a 12 month accounting period ending 31st March 2016, the maximum annual investment allowance available will be:

275/366 x £500,000   £375,683 (2016 is a leap year)
91/366   x £200,000   £49,727
Total   £425,410

If your business uses a different accounting period that straddles the 1st January 2016, then it will be entitled to a different amount of annual investment allowance. However, this can be easily calculated using the above methodology.

Moving forward, every business will be entitled to an annual investment allowance of £200,000 per year.

It Doesn't Usually Matter When You Buy Assets

Capital allowances are not usually reduced if you buy assets part way through your accounting year. This means that a sole trader with a 31st December accounting date could spend, say, £20,000 on qualifying business assets on the last day of their accounting period and reduce their taxable profits by up to £20,000.

It is also worth noting that capital allowances are reduced where the business has an accounting period of less than twelve months. This mostly affects new businesses in their first year of operation.

Tax Relief for Cars

Most capital spending is eligible for the 100% annual investment allowance. One notable exception, however, is cars. (Chapter 21 takes a detailed look at the capital allowance treatment of cars.) This is a great shame because cars are the only expensive assets many business owners purchase!

Although cars don't qualify for the annual investment allowance, vans and motorbikes do qualify (see Chapter 26).

Furthermore, certain new cars with low CO_2 emissions qualify for 'enhanced capital allowances' which also provide 100% tax relief.

Enhanced Capital Allowances

Certain categories of expenditure are eligible for 'enhanced capital allowances' of 100%. These include:

- Qualifying energy-saving equipment
  See *www.gov.uk/guidance/energy-technology-list*
- Environmentally beneficial equipment

Equipment must be new and unused to qualify for this allowance.

Enhanced capital allowance claims do not use up your annual investment allowance and are not generally subject to any monetary limit.

The 100% first-year allowance for new low-emission cars has been extended until April 2021, although the qualifying threshold will be reduced from 75g/km to 50g/km from April 2018.

The ability to claim 100% tax relief when you buy a car could prove extremely valuable. As mentioned earlier, most cars do not qualify for the annual investment allowance. Instead they usually attract much less generous writing-down allowances (see below).

So if your business buys a qualifying low CO_2 car for £20,000, the entire £20,000 expense can be offset against this year's taxable profits, with a suitable reduction for private use.

Writing-Down Allowances

Cars that do NOT have sufficiently low CO_2 emissions are only eligible for so-called 'writing down allowances'.

Similarly, if your capital spending for the year exceeds the annual investment allowance, you are only entitled to claim writing down allowances on the excess.

The writing down rate on most plant and machinery is currently 18% per year. The remaining 82% – the 'unrelieved balance' – is carried forward to your next accounting period. You can then claim further capital allowances equal to 18% of this balance.

Writing down allowances operate on the so-called 'reducing balance basis'. In other words, if you buy an asset for £10,000, your capital allowance claim is calculated as follows:

Year 1:	£10,000	x	18%	=	£1,800
Year 2:	£8,200	x	18%	=	£1,476
Year 3:	£6,724	x	18%	=	£1,211
Year 4:	£5,513	x	18%	=	£993
Year 5:	£4,520	x	18%	=	£814
Year 6:	£3,706	x	18%	=	£668
Year 7:	£3,038	x	18%	=	£547
Year 8:	£2,491	x	18%	=	£449
Year 9:	£2,042	x	18%	=	£368
Year 10:	£1,674	x	18%	=	£302

Clearly, it can take many years to claim all your tax relief. In this example, the full amount of tax relief has not been recovered even after a whole decade!

This demonstrates the value of the annual investment allowance and enhanced capital allowances. A £302 tax deduction in ten years' time is worth a lot less than a £302 tax deduction today.

Capital Allowance Pools

You do not have to calculate individual writing down allowances for every asset you own. Assets that qualify for writing down allowances are generally lumped together into something known as the 'main pool'. The main pool is effectively just a number expressed in pounds.

Example
In March 2017, Judy, a sole trader, spends £300,000 on some manufacturing equipment.

The first £200,000 qualifies for 100% tax relief thanks to the annual investment allowance. The remaining £100,000 qualifies for an 18% writing down allowance of £18,000. The unrelieved balance of £82,000 becomes her main pool.

The Special Rate Pool

Some types of capital spending are only eligible for an even more stingy 8% writing down allowance.

These assets form what is known as the 'special rate pool'.

Most small businesses only have to worry about this 8% writing down allowance if they buy a business car with CO_2 emissions of over 130g/km (110g/km from April 2018).

(You can check your car's CO_2 emissions on a variety of websites such as *www.carfueldata.direct.gov.uk*)

Certain other types of expenditure must be allocated to the special rate pool instead of the main pool. These include:

- Certain defined categories of 'integral features'.

- Expenditure of £100,000 or more on plant and machinery with an anticipated working life of 25 years or more.

- Expenditure on thermal insulation of an existing building used in a qualifying trade.

Tax Tip

If your investment spending exceeds the annual investment allowance, it is better to receive the main 18% capital allowance rate on the remainder, rather than the 8% special rate.

Fortunately, the annual investment allowance can be allocated to spending on special rate items (except cars) in preference to spending that qualifies for the normal writing down allowance rate.

This makes it more likely that any spending in excess of the annual investment allowance will fall into the main pool and enjoy an 18% writing down allowance.

Small Pools

Where the balance on either the main or special rate pool is £1,000 or less, the full balance can be written off for tax purposes.

Selling Assets

Where any asset on which capital allowances have been claimed is later sold, a deduction is made from the pool equal to the *lower* of the:

- Sale proceeds
- Original cost

If this results in a *negative* pool balance, a balancing charge arises. A balancing charge is added to your income and taxed.

Example
Noel, a sole trader, sells an old computer that was used 100% for business purposes on eBay for £300. The computer originally cost £1,000 and qualified for the 100% annual investment allowance.

The balance in Noel's main pool is currently £0 because all of his previous asset purchases have already been written down to £0 thanks to the annual investment allowance.

Deducting the £300 sale proceeds from the £0 balance results in a negative balance of -£300. This is added to Noel's income and taxed.

In many cases, the asset being disposed of will be replaced and that replacement will fall within the annual investment allowance, so that there will still be an overall beneficial effect. Nevertheless, it may often be worth delaying the disposal of an old asset until after the end of the accounting period, especially when that asset is not immediately being replaced.

Using Business Assets Privately

Where an asset is also used *privately* by the owner of an unincorporated business, capital allowances remain available BUT are reduced to reflect the private use.

For the vast majority of business owners the most important asset used both privately and for business purposes is their car (see Chapter 21).

Other assets used both privately and for business purposes include computers and mobile phones. All such assets must each be placed in their own capital allowances pool, or 'puddle', as we like to call them.

The great advantage (or occasional disadvantage) is that a balancing allowance (or charge) will arise when each asset is sold.

Balances of £1,000 or less in 'puddles' cannot be written off like similar small balances in the main or special rate pools.

The annual investment allowance is available on assets (other than cars) with an element of private use. The allowance is, however, restricted to reflect the private use, so it should be allocated to other expenditure first whenever possible.

Assets purchased for a business proprietor's own use can only attract allowances if genuinely used in the business.

Where the asset is provided to an *employee* of an unincorporated business, capital allowances are available in full but the employee will be subject to a taxable benefit in kind in respect of the private use.

Chapter 17

Maximising Your Capital Allowances Claim

Capital allowances can generate considerable tax savings, so you should give careful consideration to the timing of your capital spending.

All plant and machinery allowances are given in full for the year in which qualifying expenditure occurs, even if on the final day!

In most cases, therefore, businesses will usually benefit by accelerating qualifying capital expenditure so that it falls into an earlier accounting period. Naturally, this is only worthwhile if the expenditure was going to be made fairly soon anyway. It would not be worth making speculative purchases of plant and machinery which may not be needed for some time to come.

Example
Betty's business has enjoyed bumper sales this year and she expects to make a taxable profit of £80,000. On the last day of her accounting period, Betty buys five new computers, three new printers, and some new furniture and filing cabinets. The total cost is £6,000.

This spending qualifies for the annual investment allowance and reduces Betty's taxable profits by £6,000, thereby reducing her Income Tax and National Insurance bill for the year by £2,520 (£6,000 x 42%).

Delaying Your Spending

In some cases a business may benefit by delaying qualifying capital expenditure.

Where a business has already used up the annual investment allowance for the current year but may not do so in the next year, it could be worth deferring any further qualifying expenditure to the next year.

Example

During her accounting year ending 31st March 2017, Fiona, a sole trader, has already spent over £200,000 on plant and machinery. She is now considering buying a new machine at a cost of £20,000.

If she buys the new machine by 31st March 2017, it will only be eligible for writing down allowances at 18%.

If she buys the new machine after 31st March 2017, however, 100% tax relief will be obtained straight away because she is entitled to another year's annual investment allowance.

Changes in Income

If you expect your income to change significantly, you may be able to save a lot of tax by either delaying or accelerating your capital spending.

If you expect your income to *rise* you should consider *delaying* capital spending.

If you expect your income to *fall* you should consider *accelerating* capital spending.

For example, business owners who expect to pay basic-rate tax this year (those earning £43,000 or less), but higher-rate tax next year, may benefit by delaying capital spending until next year.

Provided that the expenditure will be covered by the annual investment allowance, this will generally mean that they obtain tax relief at 42% instead of 29%.

The same principle applies to high income earners. Those who expect to have taxable income of less than £150,000 this year, but more than £150,000 next year, will generally obtain tax relief at 47% instead of 42% by delaying their capital spending.

Anyone expecting to earn taxable income of between £100,000 and £122,000 this year should not generally delay capital spending. Those who fall into this income band face a marginal tax rate of 62%.

As a result, every additional £1 of tax deductible spending will save them 62p in tax.

The commercial implications of any delay or acceleration in qualifying capital expenditure will need to be weighed up against the potential tax savings.

More Points on Timing

Assets bought on hire purchase must be brought into use in the business by the accounting date. Merely purchasing them by that date is not enough. (See Chapter 19 for more on hire purchase.)

Assets bought on credit terms where payment is due four months or more after the purchase may not produce an immediate right to capital allowances.

Capital Allowance Disclaimers

Most capital allowances (except balancing allowances) on plant and machinery or cars may be 'disclaimed'. In fact, any proportion of the available allowance from zero to 100% may be claimed in each tax year.

Any 'disclaimed' element of the annual investment allowance or enhanced capital allowances will fall into the main pool or special rate pool, as appropriate, and will attract writing down allowances of 18% or 8%.

Disclaimers of capital allowances are useful in a number of situations where the allowance might otherwise go to waste, such as in the case of a small business whose owner has insufficient income to use their Income Tax personal allowance.

Rather than claim an allowance which will effectively be wasted, a disclaimer means that greater allowances will be available in future years.

Example
Joe has a business profit for 2016/17 of just £5,000 before capital allowances. He has no other income. During the year, he bought a new machine for £4,000 and could therefore claim an annual investment

allowance of £4,000 which would reduce his taxable profit to just £1,000.

This would be pointless, however, as Joe's profit is less than both his personal allowance and his National Insurance earnings threshold and is therefore already tax free anyway. Joe therefore disclaims his annual investment allowance in 2016/17 which means he has no capital allowance claim for the current tax year.

His expenditure of £4,000 falls into his main pool and he will be able to claim a writing-down allowance of £720 (18%) in the next tax year: 2017/18. This may not be much, but it is better than wasting his allowance altogether.

Later, Joe realises that whilst he will be paying basic rate Income Tax at 20% for 2017/18, he is likely to make enough profit to push him into the higher rate tax bracket for 2018/19.

He wonders, therefore, if he should disclaim his £720 allowance in 2017/18 in order to benefit from greater tax savings in 2018/19. Joe speaks to his accountant, Sylvia, about this but her answer is an emphatic "no!"

Sylvia explains that by disclaiming his £720 allowance in 2017/18, Joe will pay an extra £144 in Income Tax (at 20%) and £65 in National Insurance (at 9%).

"Yeah", responds Joe, "but surely I'll save much more next year when I'm paying tax at 40%".

"No, you won't", responds Sylvia. "If you claim your £720 allowance in 2017/18, you will still have unrelieved expenditure of £3,280 to carry forward and that will give you an allowance of £590 next year anyway.

The disclaimer would therefore only give you an extra allowance of £130 next year, so you'd only save £55, even with a 42% combined rate of Income Tax and National Insurance. It's just not worth it."

"Oh", says Joe. "Well, thanks for putting me straight, I don't know how I'd cope without you pulling the strings."

The lesson here is that a capital allowance disclaimer is generally worthwhile when the allowance would have gone to waste otherwise, but is seldom beneficial in other cases.

Chapter 18

How to Claim a Cashback on Capital Spending

As stated in the previous chapters, most businesses are currently entitled to immediate 100% tax relief for qualifying capital expenditure of at least £200,000 per year.

Most spending on machinery, equipment and furniture for business use qualifies for the annual investment allowance, although cars do not usually qualify (but vans usually do).

Example
Let's take Jamie, a sole trader drawing up accounts to 31st March each year. Since 1st April 2016, Jamie has bought a few small tools but has not bought any significant capital items. His forecast profits for the year ending 31st March 2017 are £75,000, which will push him well into higher rate Income Tax.

Jamie is thinking of buying some new equipment for his business at a cost of £20,000. If Jamie buys the equipment by 31st March 2017, he will be able to deduct the full cost of the equipment from his business profits, saving him £8,400 in Income Tax and National Insurance (at 40% and 2% respectively).

Jamie has a problem though. Having just paid his tax bill for the previous year on 31st January 2017, he doesn't have enough money left for the new equipment. "It's a vicious circle," he says to himself, "you pay your tax one year then can't afford the money you need to spend to avoid another big bill next year!"

Two little letters provide the answer to Jamie's problem: 'HP'.

Jamie could buy his new equipment on hire purchase and, provided that he signs the purchase contract **and** brings the equipment into use in the business by 31st March 2017, he will be entitled to 100% tax relief this year for the entire capital cost of £20,000.

(See Chapter 19 for a detailed discussion of hire purchase.)

So, for a relatively small initial outlay, Jamie will achieve his full tax saving this year.

Furthermore, having reduced his taxable profits for 2016/17 by £20,000, Jamie may have grounds to apply to reduce his self-assessment payments on account: the one that was due on 31st January 2017 and has already been paid and the one that will be due on 31st July 2017.

Therefore this will *retrospectively* reduce the tax he had to pay on 31st January 2017, as well as reducing the instalment due on 31st July.

If Jamie's current year profits are less than last year's, he is likely to be able to claim an immediate tax repayment or, if you like, a 'cashback', of £4,200:

£20,000 x 42% tax = £8,400
£8,400/2 = £4,200 reduction in the first payment on account

That should sort out the HP payments on the equipment for a few months!

Part 6

Leasing vs Buying Business Assets

Chapter 19

Hire Purchase:
How to Maximise Your Tax Relief

An important choice that many business owners face when acquiring new machinery, equipment, or other assets for use in their business is whether to lease or buy.

The decision gets further complicated by additional choices, such as whether to purchase outright or through hire purchase (HP) or, if leasing, what form of lease to take.

Cashflow is usually a major factor and this will often rule out an outright purchase, leaving the business owner to choose between HP and leasing.

In this chapter we take a look at HP: how it's treated for tax purposes and how to get the most out of the deductions available.

What Is Hire Purchase?

Under an HP agreement, you technically only hire the equipment for the term of the agreement and then have an option to buy it at the end of that period.

Typically, there will be a small additional charge added to your last payment which is the fee for exercising your purchase option and gives you legal ownership of the asset.

For tax purposes, you are treated as if you had purchased the asset at the beginning of the HP agreement. This has the advantage of providing tax relief via the capital allowances system.

Any agreement which gives you legal title to an asset at the end of its term, or which gives you an option to purchase the asset at that time for a modest additional fee, is treated as HP for tax purposes, regardless of what the agreement is actually called.

Many so-called 'lease purchase' agreements are therefore treated as HP for tax purposes.

As well as claiming capital allowances on the purchase price of an asset acquired under HP, you will also be able to claim a tax deduction for the interest charges arising under the agreement.

Until recently, there were several acceptable methods for calculating the interest charges arising in each period, including:

- The actuarial method
- Straight line
- The 'Rule of 78'

However, recent changes in accounting rules mean that the actuarial method should now be used whenever possible. This is the most accurate method and reflects the true allocation of the interest costs arising. It is, however, extremely difficult to calculate so, in practice, it will generally only be possible to use this method where the finance company has provided the appropriate details.

Failing the actuarial method, the 'Rule of 78' will now be the correct method to use for accounting purposes as it provides a good approximation of the true interest cost arising in each period. This is good news since, when compared with the simple, but crude, straight line method, it accelerates tax relief quite considerably.

Example
Moffat buys a new machine under HP. The cash purchase price of the machine is £12,300 and the total interest charge is £3,000. The business pays 36 monthly instalments of £425 (total £15,300) plus an administration charge of £50 which is added to the first instalment and an option fee of £50 which is added to the last instalment.

(Being quite small amounts, I would generally simply claim each of the two additional fees of £50 as an additional finance cost when they are paid.). The business allocates the interest cost using the 'Rule of 78'. This is done as follows:

i) Allocate a number to each instalment in reverse order. Hence, in this case, the first instalment is allocated 36; the second is allocated 35; and so on until the last instalment is allocated 1.

ii) Add up all these numbers (36+35+34+.....+2+1). In this case, this comes to 666.

iii) For each instalment, you multiply the total interest charged under the agreement by the number allocated under (i) above and then divide it by the number you got at (ii) above. This gives you the interest charge within that instalment.

Using this method the interest charge within the first instalment is:

$$£3,000 \times 36/666 = £162.16$$

The interest charge within the second instalment is:

$$£3,000 \times 35/666 = £157.66$$

Continuing in this way for the first twelve instalments, we get total interest charges of £1,648.65 in the first year of the agreement. In other words, using the 'Rule of 78' provides 65% more tax relief for interest arising in the first year than the simple straight line method. (Just in case you are wondering why it is called the 'Rule of 78', it is because the numbers 1 to 12 add up to 78. It is not, as I thought when I was a student, because it was invented in 1978!)

Accrued Interest

Most businesses remember to claim the interest charges within the HP instalments paid during the period but it is also perfectly legitimate to claim a further amount for accrued interest within the next instalment. I will explain this further by returning to our example.

117

Example Revisited

Moffat has a 31ˢᵗ March year end and actually purchased his new machine on 4ᵗʰ April 2016. His HP payments are due on the 4ᵗʰ of each month, commencing 4ᵗʰ May 2016. For the year ending 31ˢᵗ March 2017, he therefore claims all of the interest within his first 11 instalments (total £1,536.04 using the 'Rule of 78'). He can also claim accrued interest of £98.08, representing 27/31sts of the interest charge within his twelfth instalment due on 4ᵗʰ April 2017.

In summary, Moffat is able to claim the following amounts in the year ending 31ˢᵗ March 2017:

Annual investment allowance	£12,300 (purchase price*)
Interest paid	£1,536.04
Interest accrued	£98.08
Finance charge	£50.00
Total	£13,984.12

* Assuming sufficient allowance is available

HP and Capital Allowances

One critical point about an asset acquired under HP is that it is only eligible for capital allowances if it is brought into use in the business before its accounting date.

In one case a few years ago, a haulage firm with a 31ˢᵗ March year end purchased some new trucks on HP just before its year end but only bought road fund licences (tax discs) for them from 1ˢᵗ April.

HMRC pounced on this apparent error and stated that capital allowances could not be claimed in the year of purchase as the trucks were clearly not yet in use in the business as at 31ˢᵗ March.

Fortunately, however, the firm's accountant was able to point out that the trucks had been used internally, within the firm's own site, on 31ˢᵗ March, so the capital allowances were due in the earlier year after all.

The lesson is clear – make sure you bring HP assets into use before your year end.

Chapter 20

Leasing Assets

In the previous chapter we looked at the tax treatment of assets bought on hire purchase (HP). In this chapter, we will take a look at the tax considerations applying to finance leases and then take a look at the comparative merits of each method.

What Is a Finance Lease?

In practical day-to-day terms, holding an asset under a finance lease is very much the same as buying an asset on HP.

The lessee is treated as if they owned the asset (for the period of the lease), is generally free to use it as they please (subject to any restrictions under the lease) and is responsible for repairs, maintenance and running costs.

The key difference between a finance lease and HP is that the lease does not include an option or right to purchase the asset at the end of its term or, if it does, it is at a more commercial price and not the notional £50 or so found in a typical HP agreement.

In other words, it is far from certain that the lessee will purchase the asset at the end of the lease. (Whilst it is not absolutely certain that a hirer will buy an asset under a HP agreement, it is pretty likely, in view of the negligible size of the option price in most cases.)

Under a finance lease, you are not treated as owning the asset for tax purposes during the period of the lease and cannot claim capital allowances on it during that time (except in the case of some leases of five or more year's duration, known as 'long funding leases').

Instead, you may generally claim your lease payments, including any finance element, with a 15% disallowance for cars with CO_2 emissions in excess of 130g/km (110 g/km from April 2018).

You are, however, required to follow generally accepted accounting practice when claiming your lease payments. This means that, in theory, you should account for the leased asset as if it were a fixed asset of your business and then charge both the depreciation on that asset and the interest under the finance lease in your accounts in the same way as you would for an asset held on HP.

When calculating the interest charge, you should use either the actuarial method or the 'Rule of 78', as discussed in the previous chapter.

The depreciation on the leased asset, unusually, will be allowed for tax purposes.

Companies must follow these rules when preparing their accounts. Most unincorporated businesses tend to ignore them and simply claim finance lease payments as they arise, with perhaps an accrual for part of the next payment due after their accounting date (e.g. if the next payment is due 10 days after a 31st December accounting date, they would claim 21/31sts of that payment as an accrual).

This simple approach will generally be acceptable if the lease payments arise evenly over the period of the lease but should not be used if there are any 'balloon payments' (a larger payment at either the beginning or end of the lease).

The theoretical approach outlined above is, however, open to all businesses and is worth considering as it can create some timing advantages.

Firstly, as we saw in the previous chapter, there is the ability to accelerate the relief for the interest element by using the 'Rule of 78'.

Secondly, relief for the capital element can be accelerated by using a depreciation policy based on the 'reducing balance', rather than 'straight line'.

Example
Bilbo takes out a finance lease over a new piece of machinery which has a purchase price of £20,000. He has an option to purchase the machine for £5,000 at the end of his three year lease (but he has no intention of doing so as, in his view, it will not be worth that much by then).

120

Bilbo pays £500 per month over the life of the lease: a total of £18,000.

Simply claiming the lease payments as they arise (generally acceptable if Bilbo is not running his business through a company) would give him a tax deduction of £6,000 (12 x £500) for each year of the lease.

Instead, however, Bilbo could claim the £3,000 interest element of the lease using the 'Rule of 78'. This would give him a deduction of £1,649 for the interest alone in the first year of the lease.

At the same time, Bilbo could also charge depreciation on the capital value of the asset (£20,000) at the rate of 37% on the reducing balance basis. This would produce an allowable deduction of £7,400 in the first year of the lease.

(Why 37%? This rate will reduce the machine's written down value in the accounts to £5,001 after three years – a good reflection of its actual commercial value at that time.)

In total, therefore, Bilbo will actually be claiming deductions of over £9,000 for the first year of the lease – 50% more than if he had simply claimed the lease payments.

The depreciation policy used must be reasonable and, if the business has other similar assets, the same depreciation rate would usually be expected to be used on all of them. Nonetheless, as we can see, it is well worth going to the effort of following this more complex method rather than simply claiming lease payments as they are due.

HP v Finance Leases

So, now that we have looked at the tax treatment of both financing methods, we come back to our original question: 'lease or buy', what is better, HP or finance lease?

As we have seen, the treatment of the interest or finance costs is broadly similar, so it all comes down to the capital value of the asset itself.

At this point, we need to distinguish cars from other assets used in the business. We will come back to cars in Chapter 27. For the moment, we will concentrate on other assets, such as computers, furniture, equipment, machinery, vans and trucks.

Where the expenditure on these items qualifies for capital allowances then, at present, the first £200,000 of such expenditure in a year will qualify for immediate 100% tax relief under the annual investment allowance. A higher allowance may be available if your accounting period straddles 1st January 2016 – see Chapter 16.

Let's take Bilbo. If he buys his machine under HP, he will probably be able to claim an immediate deduction of £20,000. If he sells it three years later for £5,000, he may only have to deduct this amount from his main pool. At worst, he will have a balancing charge of up to £5,000.

If he leases the machine under a finance lease then, as we have seen, his allowable depreciation charge in the first year would, at best, be just £7,400.

From a tax perspective then, HP seems to come out a clear winner: where the annual investment allowance is available.

Where an asset purchase is not covered by the annual investment allowance then, in most cases, it will attract a writing down allowance at the rate of just 18%.

In Bilbo's case, this would have given him a tax deduction of just £3,600 in the first year: less than half of the allowable depreciation charge which he could have deducted if he had used a finance lease.

In Summary

From a tax perspective alone, it is generally better to purchase machinery and equipment under HP rather than lease it under a finance lease: provided that the purchase price will be covered by the annual investment allowance.

Where the annual investment allowance is not available, however, a finance lease will provide better tax relief.

Finally, however, remember that we have only been looking at tax issues here. In practice, there are many other considerations to take into account: including the fact that you get to keep an asset bought on hire purchase, but a leased asset usually has to go back to the leasing company one day.

Finance Lease v Operating Lease

Finance leases differ from 'operating leases', where you simply hire a piece of equipment for a pre-determined period and have none of the risks or rewards of ownership (e.g. you are not responsible for maintenance). Rent paid under an operating lease is simply allowed as it is paid and is a very different 'kettle of fish' to finance lease or HP payments.

Part 7

Motoring Expenses

Chapter 21

Capital Allowances - Cars

The capital allowance rules for cars are quite complex but we are confident that you will have a solid grasp of them once you have finished reading this chapter.

And, the more you understand, the more tax you will save!

Remember capital allowances reduce your taxable profits and therefore reduce your tax bill.

As we shall see, the current capital allowance rules for cars used by *self-employed* business owners (sole traders and partnerships) are far more generous than the rules for cars owned by *companies*. This is because the self employed are usually entitled to a much bigger tax deduction when they sell or trade-in their old cars.

The focus of this tax guide is the self-employed business owner, so we will not spend too much time discussing the capital allowance rules for companies.

However, the company rules are still worth mentioning because when a sole trader or partnership provides a car to an *employee* (i.e. someone who works in the business but is not an owner), the car is treated like a company car.

So in businesses owned by sole traders or partnerships the capital allowance treatment varies according to whether the car is used by:

- The self-employed business owner, or
- An employee of the business

Furthermore, it is also important to understand the company car rules if you are thinking about converting your business from sole trader or partnership status into a company. If you form a company you will no longer be self employed. Instead, you will become a company employee and, if the company provides you with a car, it will then be taxed as a company car.

Older Cars

Cars purchased **and** brought into use in the business before 6th April 2009 are subject to a slightly different set of rules. We do not cover those rules in this guide.

'Purchase' and 'Sale'

Note that, throughout this chapter, when we talk about the date that a car is 'purchased' what we are really talking about is the date you start to use the car in your business.

In other words, if you purchased a car in 2014, but only started using it for business purposes on 1st April 2016, the car will be treated as if it had been purchased on 1st April 2016 for its market value on that date.

Similarly, if you cease to use a car in your business, but do not actually dispose of it, then it must also be treated as if it had been sold for its market value on the date that you ceased to use it in your business.

A car which is 'written off' is treated as sold for the amount of insurance proceeds received.

Cars Used by the Self-Employed Business Owner

The size of your capital allowance claim depends on the car's CO_2 emissions, measured in grams of CO_2 per kilometre (g/km):

- Over 130g/km   8% allowance

- Over 75g/km but not over 130g/km   18% allowance

- 75g/km or less   100% allowance

You can check car CO_2 emissions easily using websites such as *www.carfueldata.direct.gov.uk* and *www.comcar.co.uk*.

The CO_2 emission thresholds were higher in previous tax years. In other words, it has become harder and harder to qualify for the higher capital allowance rates.

Note that a car which qualified for the 18% rate under a higher CO_2 emission threshold which applied when it was first purchased in the past will continue to enjoy that rate, as long as it is still used in the business, even if its CO_2 emissions now exceed the current threshold.

Changes Ahead

From 1st April 2018, only cars with CO_2 emissions of 50g/km or less will be eligible for the 100% allowance. This allowance will cease to be available altogether after 31st March 2021.

The threshold for the 18% rate will reduce from 130g/km to 110g/km with effect from 1 April 2018.

What Can Be Claimed?

For newly acquired cars your capital allowance claim is based on the cost of the vehicle, plus any extras. The car can be new or second hand – unless you are claiming the 100% enhanced capital allowance which only applies to new cars.

You cannot recover any VAT paid when you buy a car, even if your business is VAT registered. VAT can only be recovered on vans and motorbikes (see Chapters 24 and 26).

This means your capital allowance claim is based on the total cost, including VAT.

When you introduce a car into your business that was purchased at some point in the past, your capital allowance claim is based on the market value of the vehicle on the date it is introduced into your business.

Personalised number plates can also qualify for capital allowances in certain circumstances.

Whether the number plate is acquired to promote the business or you personally is the key factor. For example, Bill Gates might claim relief for 'M1 CRO' but not for 'BG 1'.

Private Use Tax Tip

If a car used by a self-employed business owner has NO private use, it is treated like a company car for capital allowance purposes. The rules for company cars are much less generous than the rules for cars used by self-employed business owners (except where the 100% enhanced capital allowance is available).

Cars with absolutely no private use are rare but, if your car really has no private use, our advice is: take it to the shops once a year, claim 99% business use and avoid company car tax treatment!

If your car has some private use its capital allowance claim will be reduced to reflect the vehicle's private use. However, when the car is eventually sold, you will usually be entitled to a special balancing allowance (a tax deduction). Company cars are not eligible for this special tax deduction.

Before we explain what happens when the car is sold, let's take a look at how your capital allowance claim is calculated when your car is used privately. This is best illustrated with an example.

Example
Gordon is a sole trader and buys a new car for £25,000 in June 2016. The car has CO2 emissions of 175g/km and 75% business use.

In year 1 Gordon will be entitled to a capital allowance of £1,500:

£25,000 x 8% writing down allowance = £2,000
£2,000 x 75% business use = £1,500

The amount carried forward to year 2 (the unrelieved balance) is £23,000:

£25,000 - £2,000 = £23,000

Note that the amount carried forward is £25,000 less £2,000; not £25,000 less £1,500. The amount carried forward (£23,000), is also sometimes known as the car's 'tax written down value'.

Example Continued
In year 2 Gordon will be entitled to a capital allowance of £1,380:

£23,000 x 8% writing down allowance = £1,840
£1,840 x 75% business use = £1,380

The amount carried forward to year 3 is £21,160:
£23,000 - £1,840 = £21,160

... and so on

It is important to point out that cars used privately by self-employed business owners are treated as separate, stand-alone assets. They are not lumped together with other assets in the main pool or special rate pool. This allows them to enjoy special tax treatment when they are sold.

Selling the Car

When the car is sold, a balancing allowance is available if the car is sold for less than its tax written down value. This is usually the case because most cars lose value at a faster rate than 8% per year!

A balancing allowance essentially makes up for any shortfall in the car's capital allowances. The balancing allowance reduces your taxable profits and therefore reduces your tax bill.

For cars purchased after 5th April 2009, a balancing allowance is only available if the car has both business AND private use.

Example Continued
Gordon's unrelieved balance carried forward to year 3 is £21,160. In year 3 Gordon sells the car for just £10,000. This gives rise to a balancing allowance of £8,370:

£21,160 - £10,000 = £11,160
£11,160 x 75% business use = £8,370

This means Gordon can claim a tax deduction of £8,370 in year three, saving him £3,515 in tax (at 42%) if he is a higher-rate taxpayer.

Key Result

This example illustrates one of the key differences between sole traders/partnerships and companies.

Even though Gordon, a sole trader, is only allowed to claim a capital allowance of 8% per year for this type of car, he can claim a big catch-up tax deduction when he sells the car.

Gordon would not be able to claim this balancing allowance if he was operating a company. Instead, the company would have to continue claiming tax relief at just 8% per year on the shortfall in the car's capital allowances (£11,160 in this case).

Sole traders and partnerships are also not able to claim these big catch-up tax deductions for cars given to their employees or if their own cars have no private use.

Before we leave the subject of balancing adjustments on a car's sale, we should just point out that, if a sole trader or partner's car (with private use) is sold for more than its tax written down value, a balancing charge arises. This charge is added to the business's taxable profits and is then subject to Income Tax and National Insurance at the usual rates.

A balancing charge is designed to compensate for the excess capital allowances given on the car. The amount of the charge is the difference between the car's sale proceeds and its tax written down value, with a proportionate reduction to reflect the car's private use.

Calculating Business Use

In the above example, Gordon's car had 75% business use. How do you calculate a car's business usage?

This will depend on the number of miles travelled on 'business journeys' versus the total miles travelled.

In Chapter 11 we explain what is meant by the term business journey. This is an important topic if you want to maximise your tax relief when you travel by car, train, taxi or by any other means.

For capital allowance purposes an estimated *average* proportion tends to be used as accurate business mileage figures differ from one year to the next. The proportion claimed should be reviewed if there is a major change in the car's general usage pattern.

Cars Used By <u>Employees</u> of the Business

A car provided to an employee of an unincorporated business (i.e. someone who is not an owner of the business) attracts writing down allowances at the same rate as a car used by the owner of the business, based on the car's CO_2 emissions, as set out above.

However, the key thing to remember is that cars used by employees are not treated as separate stand-alone assets. Cars entitled to an 18% writing down allowance are added to the main pool. Cars entitled to an 8% writing down allowance are added to the special rate pool (See Chapter 16 for an explanation of 'pools').

This means that when the car is sold there will NOT be a big balancing allowance to help reduce your business tax bill.

Instead, the outstanding balance remaining after deducting the car's sale proceeds will continue to attract capital allowances at 8% or 18%, along with other assets inside the pool.

Chapter 22

Motor Vehicle Running Costs

In Chapter 11 we explained what a tax-deductible business journey is.

If some of your business journeys take place in your own motor vehicle (e.g. a car, van or motorbike), then your motoring expenses will be tax deductible.

Motoring expenses come in two forms:

- The cost of the vehicle itself
- The running costs (fuel, insurance etc)

Tax relief is available for the cost of the vehicle in the form of capital allowances. These are discussed in detail in Chapter 21 for cars and Chapter 26 for other vehicles.

In this chapter, we focus on the tax relief available for vehicle running costs.

The Costs You Can Claim

Almost all the costs of running the vehicle are tax deductible:

- Fuel
- Repairs and maintenance (servicing, MOT, oil, tyres, etc)
- Insurance
- Road fund licence (aka Vehicle Excise Duty or 'Tax Disc')
- Breakdown cover (AA, RAC, etc)
- Warranty cover
- Interest on a loan or other finance to purchase the vehicle

Warranty cover needs to be spread over the life of the warranty but still ranks as an 'annual cost'. For example, for a three year warranty costing £900, claim £300 a year for three years.

Parking fines and other penalties incurred by business owners cannot be claimed under general principles.

The cost of reimbursing an employee's parking fine will normally be allowed, although this can give rise to a benefit in kind charge unless the vehicle is registered in the employer's name. It is important, however, that the penalty notice is affixed to the vehicle and not handed to the employee.

How Much Can You Claim?

As a self-employed business owner you can claim the business element of the cost of running a car. The business element is found by comparing the number of miles of business travel with the total miles travelled in the year. (See Chapter 11 for a detailed explanation of 'business travel'.)

Example
Patrick drives a total of 12,000 miles in the year, 7,000 of which are business travel. The total annual running costs of his car are £3,000, so he is able to claim £1,750:

$$7,000/12,000 \text{ x } £3,000 = £1,750$$

Mileage Logs

The recommended method for determining your business mileage is to keep an accurate record, i.e. a 'mileage log'. For each journey you should record:

- The date
- The purpose of the journey (business or private)
- Your start point
- Destination
- Miles travelled and the car's total mileage at the end of the journey.

In practice, the same level of detail is not required for your private journeys, as long as you know your total annual mileage and have the details of your business journeys.

As we know from Chapter 11, normal home to work commuting is not classed as business travel for tax purposes.

Does Everyone Keep A Mileage Log?

A mileage log is strongly recommended and is usually the only approach which HM Revenue & Customs (HMRC) is happy to accept in the event of an enquiry.

In practice, however, many people find it difficult to keep an accurate log (you've just driven 50 miles in pouring rain, you're already half an hour late for an important meeting and HMRC expects you to stop and fill in your mileage log first).

In these cases, a reasonable estimate of the car's proportionate business mileage is often used and is usually acceptable. However, if you do not keep a log you have to accept that, in the event of an enquiry, HM Revenue and Customs will often seek to reduce the business proportion.

Fixed Mileage Rates

As an alternative to claiming a suitable proportion of running costs, sole traders and business partners can instead claim fixed mileage rates for business travel in their own motor vehicle.

For cars, the mileage rates applying are 45p per mile for the first 10,000 business miles per year and 25p per mile thereafter. (See Chapter 26 for the rates applying to vans and motor cycles.)

This alternative method is now available to all sole traders and business partners (except for partnerships which include a company or other 'non-natural person' as a member).

A mileage log is essential to support a claim for business mileage (although a log is always advisable in any case).

A mileage claim also takes the place of any capital allowances claim on the vehicle, although relevant loan interest may still be allowed, where applicable.

The business owner may choose whether to adopt this approach or not but, once the decision has been taken whether to claim actual costs or business mileage rates, the same approach must then be applied throughout the life of that car. We look at the pros and cons of this approach in Chapter 23.

Employees

If your business has employees, the basic choices are:

i)   The employer owns the car and pays for everything

ii)   The employer owns the car but the employee pays for fuel

iii)   The employee owns the car and claims business mileage from the employer

Under options (i) and (ii), the car is always referred to as a 'company car', even when the employer is a sole trader or partnership.

The best choice depends on the facts of each individual case and needs to be reviewed on a 'car by car' basis.

Under option (i), the business obtains tax relief for all the car's running costs. The employee is taxed on a benefit in kind. For 2016/17, this is generally equal to somewhere between 7% and 37% of the car's original list price, depending on the car's CO_2 emissions. A further benefit in kind equal to the same percentage of £22,200 is charged in respect of fuel. The business must also pay Class 1A National Insurance at 13.8% on both charges.

This option is generally only worth considering for a 'perk' car – where the car has very little business use and high private mileage.

Option (ii) can often be the best choice where the employee has medium to high levels of business mileage.

The employee is still subject to the benefit in kind charge on the car itself, but avoids the further charge for fuel.

The business may claim tax relief for all of the running costs which it continues to incur and may also claim relief for any business mileage payments which it makes to the employee in respect of fuel used on business journeys.

The employee is not taxed on the business mileage payments they receive from the employer – provided that these do not exceed the approved rates published by HMRC. Any payments in excess of these approved rates will be subject to Income Tax and National Insurance in the same way as additional salary payments: unless the employer can demonstrate that the actual cost of business travel is genuinely higher than the approved rates.

The approved mileage rates in this case are somewhat lower than those for a small business owner using their own car for business, as they are only intended to reimburse the fuel cost, rather than the car's total running costs.

The current mileage rates (effective from 1st June 2016) applying to the reimbursement of fuel costs incurred by an employee driving a company car on business are as follows:

Engine size	Fuel Type		
	Petrol	Diesel	LPG
1,400cc or less	10p	9p	7p
1,401cc to 1,600cc	13p	9p	9p
1,601cc to 2,000cc	13p	10p	9p
Over 2,000cc	20p	12p	13p

These rates are reviewed quarterly: on 1st March, 1st June, 1st September and 1st December each year. Employers may continue to operate the previous rates for up to a month after the date of change if they wish.

The current rates can be found at:
www.gov.uk/government/publications/advisory-fuel-rates

Where the employer makes business mileage payments at a lower rate than these approved rates, the employee may claim tax relief for any shortfall.

Option (iii) is significantly different in that the employee owns the car personally. As such, the business has no running costs to claim (nor capital allowances), except for any business mileage payments which it makes to the employee.

The employee may receive tax-free business mileage payments of up to 45 pence per mile for the first 10,000 business miles in each tax year and 25 pence per mile thereafter.

Where the employer makes business mileage payments at a lower rate than these approved rates, the employee may again claim tax relief for any shortfall.

Employers may also make an additional payment of up to 5p per mile where an employee undertaking a business journey in their own car carries another employee of the business as a passenger (the journey must also qualify as a business journey for the passenger). However, unlike the main 45 pence or 25 pence rates above, the employee may not claim tax relief for any shortfall.

Option (iii) will often be preferable where a car has high business mileage and little private use. However, the choice between (ii) and (iii) is a difficult one and depends on the many factors set out above, as well as others, such as fleet insurance and VAT.

Company cars can often be insured more cheaply using fleet discounts. These discounts will only generally apply under options (i) and (ii) above and should therefore be taken into account in making a decision which option to use.

Employees Repaying Private Fuel Costs

In many businesses where option (ii) is being used, the business will pay the full cost of fuel in the first instance and then require the employee to repay the cost of private travel (rather than the employee paying for all fuel and then claiming business mileage payments from their employer).

Whilst this is often more convenient, and is better cashflow for the employees, it is essential that the full cost of private fuel is reimbursed by the employee. Otherwise they will be subject to the fuel benefit charge: which could amount to as much as £8,214 (£22,200 x 37%) at 2016/17 rates.

HMRC will usually accept that the employee has borne the full cost of private fuel where they reimburse private mileage at the approved rates set out above, or greater. Exceptions may arise in the case of cars with engine capacities in excess of three litres.

Reimbursement at less than the approved rates will not be acceptable unless the employer can demonstrate that the actual cost of private travel is genuinely being covered.

Chapter 23

How to Increase Tax Relief on Motoring Costs

Small self employed business owners have an important tax planning decision to make when it comes to motoring costs.

If you make the right choice you could enjoy thousands of pounds of additional tax relief.

As we know self-employed individuals who use their cars for business purposes are entitled to claim tax relief on a percentage of their motoring expenses.

Motoring expenses come in two forms:

- The cost of the vehicle itself
- The running costs

Tax relief is available for the cost of the vehicle in the form of capital allowances. Running costs include fuel, repairs, insurance etc.

The percentage of motoring expenses on which self-employed business owners can claim tax relief is found by comparing the number of business miles travelled during the year with the total miles travelled.

The Alternative Route

As explained in Chapter 22, most business owners can alternatively choose to ignore their actual motoring expenses and claim tax relief at the following fixed business mileage rates instead:

- 45p per mile (first 10,000 miles)
- 25p per mile thereafter

Example

Patrick is a self-employed consultant who earns fees of £65,000 per year. He travels 12,000 miles per year on business and 20,000 miles per year in total. Instead of claiming 60% of his actual motoring costs, Patrick can claim tax relief as follows on his 12,000 business miles:

- *10,000 x 45p = £4,500*
- *2,000   x 25p = £500*

Patrick's total tax deduction for the year will be £5,000.

If you want to calculate your motoring tax deduction using these business mileage rates, you cannot then claim either your actual running costs or capital allowances for the vehicle.

Whichever approach you adopt, you must apply it throughout the life of the car.

So the content of this chapter may only become relevant when you buy your next car and can choose a new tax calculation method.

Simplicity versus Tax Savings

So which approach is best: mileage rates or actual expenses?

Many self-employed business owners may opt to calculate their tax deduction using the 45p and 25p business mileage rates because this method is supposedly simpler: you don't have to type up all your petrol receipts and other running costs or calculate capital allowances.

However, the amount of time saved may be exaggerated because you will still have to keep a log of your business mileage recording the date, purpose of the journey, start point, destination and miles travelled.

Maximising Tax Relief

The more important question is: Which method produces the biggest tax deduction, i.e. the most tax relief?

Sometimes your actual motoring expenses will produce the biggest tax deduction, sometimes the mileage rates – it all depends on your personal circumstances.

The amounts at stake are potentially significant and could amount to thousands of pounds per year.

The two most important factors influencing your choice are arguably:

- The cost of your car
- The amount of business mileage

The more expensive your car is, the more important it is to claim capital allowances, which means you will also claim your actual motoring costs.

The more you travel on business, however, the more likely you are to benefit from using the fixed mileage rates.

Example

Arthur is a sole trader with turnover of £60,000 per year. He buys a new car for £40,000. He only drives 5,000 miles per year, half of which is business travel. His total running costs are £1,940 per year. He sells the car three years later for £16,000.

If he uses the fixed mileage rates the total tax deduction over the three year period will be: 5,000 miles x 50% business x 45p x 3 years = £3,375.

If he claims his actual motoring costs, his capital allowances claim will be £12,000 over the three year period: £40,000 - £16,000 x 50%; and his tax deduction for running costs will be £2,910: £1,940 x 3 years x 50%. His total motoring tax deduction will therefore be £14,910.

By claiming his actual motoring costs, Arthur will increase his tax deduction by £11,535!

However, claiming your actual motoring costs will not always produce the most favourable tax outcome, especially if you drive a modestly priced car and do a lot of business mileage.

Example

Terry is also a sole trader with turnover of £60,000 per year. He buys a new car for £10,000. He drives 25,000 miles per year, 75% of which is business travel. His total running costs are £4,484 per year. He sells the car three years later for £4,000.

If he uses the fixed mileage rates the total tax deduction over the lifetime of the car will be a sizeable £20,063:

10,000 miles x 45p x 3 years = £13,500
8,750 miles   x 25p x 3 years = £6,563

If he claims his actual motoring costs, his capital allowances claim will be a paltry £4,500 over the three year period: £10,000 - £4,000 x 75%; and his tax deduction for running costs will be £10,089: £4,484 x 3 x 75%. His total motoring tax deduction will therefore be £14,589.

By using the 45p and 25p mileage rates, Terry will increase his tax deduction by £5,474.

Chapter 24

How to Save VAT on Your Motoring Costs

If your business is VAT registered it's essential to understand the special VAT rules for motoring costs so that you maximise your tax relief.

Reclaiming VAT on the Purchase Price

Cars

When you buy a car for use in your business the general rule is that you cannot reclaim any VAT. There are exceptions, however, including taxis, driving school cars and hire cars.

You can also recover the VAT if the car is used exclusively for business purposes and is not available for any private use. How do you convince the taxman that a car is not available for private use? With difficulty!

It has been argued that if there is insurance for business use only, this acts as a legal restraint on any private use, so it should be possible to reclaim VAT. However, you will probably struggle to find any insurer offering cover for business use only.

Although VAT generally cannot be recovered on cars it's interesting to note that several taxpayers have taken the taxman to court on this issue and won.

In one case (*Shaw v Revenue & Customs*) a farmer was able to reclaim VAT on a BMW X5.

The taxman argued that because the farmer's insurance also covered use for social, domestic and pleasure purposes, the vehicle was available for personal use and VAT should not be reclaimed. However, the farmer pointed out that even his combine harvester was covered for social domestic and pleasure use because it was cheaper than a policy covering business use only!

The farmer had actually purchased a second BMW X5 for private use and although the BMW bought for business use could be used privately it was very unlikely that it would be.

In summary, it is not impossible to reclaim VAT on a car BUT you would have to show some special circumstances, like our farmer with his two BMWs. The vast majority of business owners should not make a claim for VAT when they buy cars for use in their business.

Commercial Vehicles

If you are VAT registered, you can reclaim VAT on commercial vehicles. Note that if you are a sole trader or partnership business you cannot automatically reclaim the VAT on commercial vehicles – the vehicle also has to be used for business purposes.

If the vehicle is used 75% for business purposes, you can reclaim 75% of the VAT, and so on. Most smaller commercial vehicles, like vans, have at least some private use. If you claim 100% business use the taxman may not believe you!

A vehicle is a commercial vehicle if it has:

- a payload of 1 tonne or more, or
- an unladen weight of 3 tonnes or more

Obvious examples include tractors, lorries and most vans. Many double-cab pickups also fall into this category: the likes of the Volkswagon Amarok, the Mitsubishi L200 or the Ford Ranger. The manufacturer's website will tell you if the payload is more than one tonne.

Is it a Car, Is it a Van?

Some vehicles may not be able to carry a payload of one tonne but are still treated as vans for VAT purposes because they are not mainly designed for carrying passengers or do not have rear seats and windows. Try typing 'car derived vans' into Google Images for some examples.

HMRC has produced a list of car derived vans, showing whether they are classed as commercial vehicles or cars for VAT purposes.

You can find this list on the gov.uk website by typing 'car derived vans and combi vans' into Google. (*www.gov.uk/.../hm-revenue-and-customs-car-derived-vans-and-combi-vans*.) This list may not always be up to date, however, so always check with a dealer.

Motorbikes

You can reclaim VAT on a motorbike used for business purposes. Again for self-employed business owners there has to be a suitable reduction in the VAT claim if the bike also has private use.

Accessories

You generally cannot reclaim VAT on accessories (e.g. satnavs or car phone kits) that are fitted when the car is purchased. If, however, you buy an accessory later on you can reclaim all VAT if the accessory is used for business purposes.

Running Costs

Self-employed business owners normally have to reduce their VAT claims if there is any private use of an asset. However, when it comes to vehicle servicing and repair costs, there is an important exception:

You can reclaim 100% of the VAT paid on vehicle servicing and repairs, even if the vehicle is also used privately.

Example
Fiona is a VAT registered sole trader. She sends her car to the garage for its annual service and ends up with a bill of £1,000 + £200 VAT. She uses her car just 5% of the time for business purposes. She can recover 100% of the VAT (£200) and then claim 5% of the net cost for Income Tax purposes (£1,000 x 5% = £50).

Parking Costs

There is no VAT levied on the use of on-street parking meters. However, some parking charges do attract VAT, e.g. multi-storey car parks.

The VAT can be recovered if the expense is incurred when you are out and about on business, e.g. visiting customers or leaving your car at the airport.

Leasing and VAT

If you lease a vehicle and use it exclusively for business purposes, all the VAT on the lease payments can be reclaimed.

If the leased vehicle is used for both business and private purposes, you can reclaim 50% of the VAT, regardless of whether the business use is 1% or 99%.

When you are shopping around for the best deal you should ask whether the cost includes VAT or not and factor your 50% VAT reclaim into your calculations.

VAT on other charges such as servicing costs are not included in the 50% restriction and can be recovered in full.

Leasing does NOT include hire purchase – you generally cannot recover VAT on hire purchase if there is any private use (there is no VAT on the interest element in any case).

With short-term hire car contracts of less than five days duration, the VAT can be recovered in full whenever there is any business use. For contracts of five days or more, only 50% of the VAT can be recovered unless there is exclusive business use of the vehicle.

Number Plates

You can reclaim the VAT on a personalised number plate, providing the number plate was purchased for business purposes, for example to advertise the business or to create the impression of success.

Your chances of successfully reclaiming VAT are probably greater if the number plate is similar to the name of the business, rather than your own name. For example, Richard Branson would be better off going for V1 RGN, rather than RB1.

In many cases this distinction is not necessary, however, because the business's name and the owner's name are one and the same.

Your claim may be assisted by the fact that:

- Your business is trying to attract publicity locally (i.e. where the vehicle will be seen)

- The business name is readily identifiable (some number plates are too cryptic)

- The amount paid for the number plate is modest in relation to other costs of the business

VAT on Fuel

If a vehicle is used exclusively for business purposes all the VAT on fuel can be reclaimed.

If a car is used for both private and business travel, there are two main choices when it comes to reclaiming VAT on business fuel.

We take a closer look at which method is best in the next chapter.

Chapter 25

VAT on Fuel: How to Claim a Bigger Refund

If your business is VAT registered and your car is used for both private and business travel, you have two main choices when it comes to reclaiming VAT on your business fuel:

- Reclaim the VAT on **all** your fuel, but pay the Fuel Scale Charge, or

- Only claim back VAT on fuel used for business purposes

Choosing the correct method could save you hundreds if not thousands of pounds over the life of your car.

Note: Van owners cannot use the Fuel Scale Charge method. They can only claim back VAT on fuel used for business mileage.

Method #1
Fuel Scale Charge

With this method you can claim back all the VAT on your fuel, even fuel used for private, non-business travel. In return, you have to pay a Fuel Scale Charge – an amount is added to the VAT bill of the business.

The Fuel Scale Charge is a fixed charge based on your car's CO_2 emissions. If you do a lot of private mileage and reclaim all the VAT on private fuel using this method, you could save a lot of tax!

The accompanying table contains the full range of charges applicable from 1st May 2016 for businesses that submit quarterly VAT returns.

VAT – Quarterly Fuel Scale Charges

CO2 Band (g/km)	VAT
120 or less	£19.33
125	£29.17
130	£31.00
135	£32.83
140	£34.83
145	£36.83
150	£38.83
155	£40.83
160	£42.67
165	£44.67
170	£46.50
175	£48.50
180	£50.50
185	£52.33
190	£54.33
195	£56.33
200	£58.33
205	£60.33
210	£62.17
215	£64.00
220	£66.00
225 or more	£68.00

For example, if you have a car with CO_2 emissions of 150g/km the VAT due is £38.83. This amount is added to the VAT your business pays HMRC (Box 1 on your VAT return).

The actual VAT you have paid on your fuel is then reclaimed just like any other business expense (Box 4 of your VAT return).

If your car's CO_2 emissions are not a multiple of 5, you should round down to the nearest emission figure, e.g. 153g/km rounds down to 150g/km.

Method #2
Claim VAT on Business Mileage Only

With this method you simply claim back VAT on fuel that is actually used for business mileage. If you have driven 3,000 miles during the VAT quarter and 1,000 are business miles, you can recover one third of the VAT on your fuel.

If you have quite low private mileage, you may be better off using this method.

If you use this method you must keep a detailed log of your business mileage. (Remember, without an accurate mileage log HMRC will often seek to reduce your tax claim in the event of an enquiry, leading to additional tax and possibly penalties too.)

Example
Keeley, a VAT-registered sole trader, drives an executive saloon with CO2 emissions of 232g/km. The car does 28.5 miles per gallon and she does 16,000 private miles and 4,000 business miles per year.

Method #1 Fuel Scale Charge

Keeley pays extra VAT of £68 per quarter – £272 per year. Her overall VAT position is as follows:

Private mileage	*16,000*
Business mileage	*4,000*
Total Mileage	*20,000*
Total fuel cost	*£3,509*
VAT reclaimed	*£585*
Less: Scale charge	*£272*
Total VAT Relief	*£313*

Method #2
Claim VAT on Business Mileage Only

Business mileage	*4,000*
Business fuel cost	*£702*
Total VAT Relief	*£117*

Overall, method one (Fuel Scale Charge) delivers £196 more VAT relief per year than method two (claiming VAT relief on business mileage only).

More comparisons, based on different amounts of private mileage, are contained in the table below. A negative number means Keeley is better off claiming actual business mileage rather than paying the Fuel Scale Charge.

Fuel Scale Charge Savings

Private Mileage	VAT Saving
1,000	-£243
3,000	-£184
5,000	-£126
8,000	-£38
10,000	£20
13,000	£108
16,000	£196
20,000	£313

The above figures are based on an estimated average fuel cost of £1.10 per litre over the course of the year.

If Keeley's private mileage is less than around 9,300 miles she enjoys more VAT relief by basing her claim on her actual business mileage (method two).

An interesting point to note is that the savings arising are purely dependent on the amount of private mileage. The amount of business mileage is totally irrelevant – as long as there is *some* business mileage, that is!

Green Car – Low CO2 Emissions

Melody, a VAT-registered sole trader, drives a car with CO2 emissions of just 136g/km. It does 49 miles per gallon. If she pays the Fuel Scale Charge she will pay £32.83 per quarter – £131.32 per year. The table below shows her savings from using the Fuel Scale Charge instead of reclaiming VAT on her business mileage.

Private Mileage	VAT Saving
1,000	-£114
3,000	-£80
5,000	-£46
8,000	£5
10,000	£39
13,000	£90
16,000	£141
20,000	£209

The above figures are again based on an estimated average fuel cost of £1.10 per litre over the course of the year.

Company Cars

Cars provided to employees are usually called 'company cars': even when the business is not a company.

Where the business pays for all the fuel used in a company car, either of the same two methods for claiming VAT relief may be used. The employee will, however, be subject to a benefit-in-kind charge.

Where the business instead pays a mileage allowance in respect of business travel, the business can claim VAT relief on the allowance paid (i.e. one sixth of the payment, at the current 20% VAT rate).

Where an employee uses their own car for business travel and is reimbursed by the business, the business can again claim VAT relief on the fuel element within the mileage allowance paid.

HMRC publishes advisory fuel rates every quarter, which businesses can use for reimbursing fuel costs incurred by employees and as the basis for the calculation of the fuel element within mileage allowances for private cars. See Chapter 22 for further details.

HMRC will also accept rates published by motoring organisations, such as the AA and RAC, as the basis for the calculation of the fuel element within mileage allowances.

Summary

The Fuel Scale Charge produces greater VAT savings if you have high private mileage. If your private mileage is quite low, paying the Fuel Scale Charge is not worthwhile. The amounts saved may appear quite small, but remember:

- They are annual amounts. If you make the right choice now, you could save hundreds, possibly thousands of pounds, over a number of years.

- They are calculated for just one car. If you have more than one business car, your savings are multiplied accordingly.

Chapter 26

Become a Van Man and Claim the Full Monty of Tax Reliefs

When most of us think of vans, we probably picture something like a battered old Ford Transit – not really suitable for taking the kids to school or popping down to the golf club (you might even get black-balled).

But when we tell you that many of the vehicles classed as 'vans' under tax legislation are every bit as comfortable and convenient as the average modern 4 x 4, you might start to look at them in a different light.

Add in the fact that, when it comes to saving tax, vans have several major advantages over cars, and most people really sit up and take notice. Over half the cost can often be recovered in tax relief, effectively making it a much cheaper alternative to a car.

VAT

First, there's the VAT. If your business is registered for VAT, you can claim back the VAT on a van purchased for business use.

Example
Let's take two vehicles, both costing £30,000: one's a car and one's a van. Vanessa buys the van and claims back £5,000 in VAT. Carlos pays the same amount of VAT on his car but can't reclaim a penny, no matter how much he uses the car in his business.

Capital Allowances

The second big advantage is capital allowances. Vans are eligible for the annual investment allowance, which now provides immediate 100% tax relief on up to £200,000 of expenditure (more if the accounting period of the business straddles 1st January 2016 – See Chapter 16).

Most cars only attract writing-down allowances at either 8% or 18%: depending on the car's CO_2 emissions (see Chapter 21 for further details).

Some cars (currently those with CO_2 emissions of 75g/km or less) attract a 100% enhanced capital allowance but, in general, we can say that the capital allowance treatment of vans is more generous than the capital allowance treatment of cars.

Example continued

Let's suppose that Vanessa and Carlos are both sole traders using their vehicles 100% for business purposes, both are higher-rate taxpayers, and both purchase their vehicles during an accounting period of twelve months ending on 31st March 2017.

After recovering her VAT, Vanessa can claim the remaining cost of £25,000 against her profits for tax purposes. This saves her a further £10,500 (at 42%: 40% Income Tax and 2% National Insurance).

Including her VAT reclaim, Vanessa has recovered a total of £15,500, or 52% of the cost of her van. In other words, the taxman has paid over half!

Carlos's car has CO2 emissions of 163g/km, so he can only claim capital allowances at 8%. This gives him a claim of just £2,400 in the first year, saving a mere £1,008 in Income Tax and National Insurance.

Carlos will be able to claim further capital allowances in later years but, at this point, he is £14,492 worse off than Vanessa despite the fact that they bought similar vehicles for similar purposes. Vanessa's just happened to be classed as a van.

Private Use of the Vehicle

The capital allowances on both vans and cars bought by sole traders or business partners for their own use must be restricted to reflect any element of private use.

The VAT reclaim on a van with an element of private use will also need to be restricted. Even so, most of the van's advantages still remain.

Example continued

Let's suppose that Vanessa and Carlos both use their vehicles privately 25% of the time. Vanessa's VAT reclaim will be reduced to £3,750, giving her a net purchase cost for the van of £26,250.

Her capital allowances claim will then be as follows:

Annual investment allowance (75% business use)
£26,250 x 75% = £19,688

Vanessa's Income Tax and National Insurance saving will be £8,269 (£19,688 x 42%) and her total tax savings on the van will be £12,019 (£3,750 VAT plus £8,269 Income Tax and National Insurance).

Carlos's capital allowances claim will be reduced to £1,800, saving him just £756 in Income Tax and National Insurance.

Both business owners have lost some of their tax relief, but Vanessa is still more than £11,000 better off than Carlos simply because she bought a van instead of a car.

Employees

There are no restrictions for private use when a vehicle is bought by a self-employed business owner for use by an employee.

Instead, however, there is an Income Tax benefit-in-kind charge on the employee using the vehicle privately. The employer must also pay secondary National Insurance at 13.8% on the same charge.

Cars almost always have some private use and the annual benefit-in-kind charge is currently usually somewhere between 7% and 37% of the car's original list price, depending on its fuel type and CO_2 emissions level.

Example continued

Let's now suppose that Carlos's car has a diesel engine and was bought for a higher-rate taxpayer employee. For the sake of illustration, we will assume that the car's list price was £30,000. With CO2 emissions of 163g/km, the benefit-in-kind charge on the car for 2016/17 will be £9,600 (£30,000 x 32%). Carlos's employee will pay Income Tax of £3,840 (at 40%) and Carlos has to pay £1,325 in employer's National Insurance (at 13.8%).

By contrast, the annual benefit-in-kind charge for private use of a van is currently just £3,170, resulting in Income Tax of £1,268 if the employee is a higher-rate taxpayer and employer's National Insurance of just £437.

The benefit-in-kind charge on a car applies whenever there is any private use, even if it is simply available for private use and even if it is merely used for home to work travel.

Vans score again here because an employee who is only permitted to use the van for home to work travel is not subject to the benefit-in-kind charge.

Minor and incidental private use, such as stopping to buy a paper on the way home without making a significant detour, is also permitted.

Private Fuel for Employees

Further benefit-in-kind charges apply where fuel is provided to employees of the business for private use.

For cars, the charge for 2016/17 is £22,200 multiplied by the car's taxable percentage. So the charge can be as high as £8,214 (£22,200 x 37%).

This will cost a higher rate taxpayer employee £3,286 in Income Tax (at 40%) and the employer £1,134 in National Insurance (at 13.8%).

Once again, a van proves better: the private fuel charge is just £598, costing a higher rate taxpayer employee £239 a year in Income Tax and costing the employer just £83 in National Insurance.

What is a Van?

The definition of a van varies from one tax to another.

For **capital allowances**, a van is effectively a vehicle which is:

    i)   Primarily suited for the conveyance of goods or burden of any description, or

    ii)   Of a type not commonly used as a private vehicle and unsuitable to be so used.

(Before you ask – no, your children don't count as a 'burden'!)

A vehicle only needs to meet one of these criteria to qualify as a van and be eligible for 100% relief immediately on its purchase. It is important to bear this in mind because HMRC tends to think that a vehicle needs to meet both criteria to qualify as a van and often needs to be put right on this point!

For **VAT** purposes, a van is generally a vehicle which:

    i)   Can carry a maximum payload of at least one tonne, or

    ii)   Has no accommodation to the rear of the driver's seat fitted, or capable of being fitted, with side windows.

For benefit-in-kind purposes, a van is simply defined as a vehicle primarily suited for the conveyance of goods or burden.

Vehicles with a maximum laden weight over 3.5 tonnes are not classed as 'vans', but could provide even greater advantages. Not many people will want to use them for the 'school run' though!

Double-Cab Pick-Ups

One type of 'van' which has become popular in recent years is the so-called 'double-cab pick-up'. An attractive alternative to a large car, they have enough seating space for the average family and often have removable canopies which effectively make them just like a large '4 x 4' with a lot of extra storage space in the back!

Several manufacturers produce these vehicles specifically designed to carry a payload of one tonne and thus meet the VAT definition of a van. HMRC has also confirmed that it will accept these vehicles as vans for benefit-in-kind purposes. The capital allowances position is slightly less certain but few people seem to have encountered any problem to date.

It is important to ensure that the vehicle can still carry a payload of at least one tonne with its canopy attached. Broadly speaking, however, as long as this rule is met, a double-cab pick-up would seem to attract all the tax advantages of a van whilst providing all the comfort of a car.

Motorbikes

If there's not enough room on your driveway for a double-cab pick-up, you might fancy a motorbike instead. Motorbikes attract many of the same tax advantages as vans but take up a lot less space.

VAT can be reclaimed on the purchase of a motorbike used for business purposes and businesses can also claim the annual investment allowance on this expenditure – generally providing immediate 100% tax relief in most cases.

Sole traders and business partners using a motorbike personally must restrict their claims to reflect private use.

Motorbikes purchased for the use of employees will not be subject to any private use restrictions but may give rise to benefit-in-kind charges.

The annual benefit-in-kind charge is equal to 20% of the *market value* of the motorbike when first provided to the employee plus any running costs borne by the employer, including fuel.

Unlike cars and vans, however, the charge is proportionately reduced to reflect any business use. It is also worth noting that the charge is based on the motorbike's market value when first provided, not on list price, and can be reduced considerably by buying a second-hand bike.

Mileage Rates

As with cars, it is possible for sole traders and business partners to claim fixed mileage rates for business travel in their own van or on their own motorbike as an alternative to claiming the actual running costs.

The rate for vans is the same as for cars: 45p per mile for the first 10,000 business miles travelled in each tax year and 25p per mile thereafter.

For motorcycles, a single flat rate of 24p per business mile may be claimed.

When claiming these mileage rates it is important to remember that:

- Keeping a mileage log is essential (although a mileage log is advisable in any case)

- You cannot also claim any running costs or capital allowances for the vehicle; although you could still claim a suitable proportion of any finance costs, where relevant

- Once you have chosen one method or the other (i.e. either fixed mileage rates, or a proportion of actual running costs and capital allowances), you must stick to that method throughout your ownership of the vehicle

Chapter 27

Cars: Lease or Buy?

In Chapters 19 and 20, we looked at the pros and cons of buying equipment for your business under Hire Purchase (HP) or leasing it under a finance lease.

Up to now, we have looked at the general principles applying to most types of assets, such as machinery, computers, furniture and vans. Cars, however, are subject to some additional rules which mean that we need to take a slightly different approach when considering the 'lease or buy' question.

VAT

The first significant difference between cars and other business assets is the fact that businesses are generally unable to recover any of the VAT on the purchase of a car: whether under HP or not.

Where cars are held under a finance lease, the business may generally recover 50% of the VAT on the lease payments (assuming the business is registered and fully taxable for VAT purposes). This represents a major advantage for VAT registered businesses leasing cars rather than buying them.

As with most other things in the tax world, however, there are many other factors to take into account: such as the comparative merits of the finance deals available and, of course, the fact that a leased car will have to go back to the leasing company one day.

Lease Payments

Where a business asset is held under a finance lease, the business may usually claim a tax deduction for the lease payments: either by simply claiming the payments as they arise, or by claiming a combination of interest and depreciation.

For cars with CO_2 emissions in excess of 130g/km, however, a 15% disallowance must be applied to the lease payments (in other words, only 85% of the payments, or interest and depreciation charges, may be claimed for tax purposes). From April 2018 the CO_2 threshold will fall to 110g/km.

Capital Allowances

Where a car is purchased under HP it will be eligible for capital allowances. It will not, however, be eligible for the immediate 100% deduction provided by the annual investment allowance, as cars are not eligible for this allowance. However, cars with CO_2 emissions of 75g/km or less (50g/km from April 2018) are currently eligible for an immediate 100% tax deduction.

Cars with CO_2 emissions of more than 75g/km but no more than 130g/km are currently eligible for writing-down allowances of 18%; cars with CO_2 emissions of more than 130g/km are eligible for writing-down allowances of just 8%. Again, from April 2018 the above CO_2 threshold will fall from 130g/km to 110g/km.

Private Use by the Self-Employed

Where any asset is used privately by a self-employed business owner, all of the relevant Income Tax deductions must be restricted accordingly, including capital allowances, lease payments, depreciation and interest charges.

For example, where the asset has 30% private use, only 70% of the relevant deductions may be claimed.

This is equally true for any assets subject to private use but applies most commonly to cars owned by the self-employed.

No such adjustments are required in the case of assets used privately by employees, although benefit-in-kind charges will apply instead.

Private use does not affect the recovery of VAT on car lease payments, since the standard flat-rate restriction of 50% is deemed to cover this already.

Making the Decision

As with any other asset, the 'lease or buy' question for a car is dependent on a number of factors, including the relative merits of the deals available at the time. From a tax perspective, however, the factors outlined above mean that the decision is also dependent on:

- Whether the business is registered and fully taxable for VAT purposes
- The level of the car's CO_2 emissions
- The amount of private use by the proprietor

For the sake of illustration, I will now look at a 'like with like' situation where the car can either be purchased under HP or held under a finance lease at the same overall cost before considering tax.

To start off with, we'll also assume the car will have 25% private use by a sole trader who is registered and fully taxable for VAT purposes and that the car has CO_2 emissions of over 130g/km.

Example
Prianka is interested in a car which costs £30,000 to buy outright. She expects to run it for four years and it will have an estimated market value of £6,000 at the end of that time.

Prianka draws up accounts to 5th April each year and will acquire the car on 6th April 2017.

Prianka could enter an HP agreement to buy the car over four years at a total cost of £36,000. Assuming that she then sold it for £6,000 on 5th April 2021, her allowable deductions for Income Tax purposes would be as follows:

	2017/18	*2018/19*	*2019/20*	*2020/21*
Capital allowances	2,400	2,208	2,031	17,361
Interest	2,602	1,867	1,133	398
	5,002	4,075	3,164	17,759
Private use (25%)	-1,251	-1,019	-791	-4,440
Deductions	3,752	3,057	2,373	13,319

164

The interest charges included above have been calculated using the 'Rule of 78' (see Chapter 19 for details).

The total deductions claimed over the four year period amount to £22,500, which is equivalent to 75% of Prianka's total cost of £36,000 less the car's sale proceeds of £6,000.

Alternatively, Prianka could hold the car under a four-year finance lease at a total cost of £30,000. The lease payments would amount to £7,500 each year but Prianka would be able to reclaim 50% of the VAT arising, reducing her actual cost to just £6,875.

For Income Tax purposes, she would then need to disallow 15% of the net payment due to the car's high CO_2 emissions and a further 25% of the remaining 85% due to her private use of the vehicle. This would leave her able to claim a deduction of £4,383 each year, or a total of £17,532 over four years.

In this example, I have assumed that Prianka would calculate her HP interest using the 'Rule of 78', but would claim her finance lease payments as they arise. As explained in Chapter 20, however, the 'Rule of 78' also remains available for calculating the interest element of finance lease payments, and it will generally be more beneficial.

I have also chosen Prianka's accounting period and acquisition date for the car on the basis of simplicity. Buying the car on HP and bringing it into business use before the end of her previous accounting period would accelerate some of her capital allowances, but would not alter the overall outcome.

Weighing it Up

Buying the car under HP would give Prianka total Income Tax deductions of £22,500 over four years. This would save her £6,525 as a basic rate taxpayer, or £9,450 as a higher-rate taxpayer (including National Insurance).

Leasing the car would give rise to VAT repayments totalling £2,500 but Income Tax deductions of just £17,532. Prianka's total savings would then amount to £7,584 as a basic rate taxpayer, or £9,863 as a higher-rate taxpayer.

So, from a purely tax-driven point of view, we can see that Prianka would usually expect to be better off leasing her car rather than buying it under HP. Not only are the total tax savings greater, but tax relief is also obtained much earlier on average.

The same considerations will usually apply to most other sole traders or business partners acquiring a car for their own use but there are some potential exceptions to be aware of.

It could sometimes be more beneficial to buy the car under HP if the business proprietor expects to be a basic-rate taxpayer in the first few years that they own it but a higher-rate taxpayer in the year that they sell it.

A higher-rate taxpayer with no more than 10% private use of the car would be slightly better off overall if they bought it under HP. However, the slight overall saving must be weighed against the fact that most of the tax relief only arises when the car is sold.

Non-VAT Registered Traders

The position would be different if Prianka had not been registered for VAT. She would then have been unable to recover any of the VAT on her finance lease payments and would simply have claimed an Income Tax deduction of £4,781 each year (85% of £7,500 less the 25% private use adjustment).

The total deduction over four years would then be £19,124 - 15% less than the £22,500 available under HP. It is, however, important to remember that the majority of the deductions available under HP only arise when the car is sold, whereas the deductions arise evenly over the period of a finance lease (or can even be accelerated where the 'Rule of 78' is applied to the interest element; or where depreciation is calculated on a 'reducing balance' basis – see Chapter 20 for details).

Lower Emission Cars

Where the car has CO_2 emissions of more than 75g/km but not more than 130g/km, there are two important changes to take into account: a higher rate of capital allowances will be available where

166

the car is purchased under HP but there will be no 15% disallowance of finance lease payments.

Keeping the other facts the same as for Prianka, a car with CO_2 emissions at this level would give rise to the following deductions when purchased under HP:

	2017/18	2018/19	2019/20	2020/21
Capital allowances	5,400	4,428	3,631	10,541
Interest	2,602	1,867	1,133	398
	8,002	6,295	4,764	10,939
Private use (25%)	-2,001	-1,574	-1,191	-2,735
Deductions	6,002	4,722	3,573	8,204

As before, the total deductions available over the four year period amount to £22,500.

If the same car was held under a finance lease, the trader would again be able to reclaim 50% of the VAT arising, reducing their annual cost to £6,875. They could then claim an Income Tax deduction for 75% of this sum: £5,156 per year, or £20,624 over the four year period.

Hence, taking account of the £2,500 of VAT repayments, for cars with this level of emissions, finance leases again appear more beneficial in most cases for VAT-registered traders.

Where the business is not registered for VAT, the Income Tax deductions available under a finance lease would simply amount to £7,500 per year less the 25% private use adjustment, i.e. £5,625. The total deductions claimed over four years would thus amount to £22,500. Whilst this is the same total as for a similar car purchased under HP, it must again be remembered that tax relief is generally available sooner under a finance lease (and can be accelerated even further by following the advice given in Chapter 20).

In Conclusion

From a pure tax perspective alone, most businesses will be better off holding cars under finance leases rather than purchasing them under HP.

Potential exceptions include:

- Non-VAT registered businesses purchasing cars with CO_2 emissions of more than 130g/km or no more than 75g/km

- Sole traders or business partners buying cars for their own use who expect to have private use of 10% or less, or who expect to be paying a higher rate of tax when they sell the car

Remember, however, that all of this is based on tax considerations alone and takes no account of any other differences which may arise. In practice, it is essential to take account of the commercial aspects of the deals on offer, including the effective interest rates and other terms applying.

Additional Information

Proprietors Making Mileage Claims

Some sole traders and business partners claim business mileage rates rather than the actual cost of their cars (see Chapter 23).

Where the fixed mileage rates are being claimed, no other costs related to the proprietor's car can be claimed (apart from finance costs). Hence, from a tax perspective, there is generally no difference between HP and a finance lease.

Cars for Employees

Where a car is provided to an employee of any business, we call it a 'company car'.

There are no private use adjustments for company cars. For VAT registered businesses, this has the effect of reducing the value of the VAT repayment available under a finance lease relative to the value of the tax deductions available under HP. However, despite this, most VAT registered businesses will still enjoy a greater overall saving by holding employees' cars under finance leases.

It is only in the case of a higher-rate taxpayer sole trader (or partnership made up of higher-rate taxpayers) acquiring a car with CO_2 emissions in excess of 130g/km for use by an employee, that the ultimate savings available under HP may eventually exceed those available under a finance lease.

Even then, the fact that there will be no balancing adjustment on the sale of the car means that it will usually take a very long time before the tax deductions available under HP outweigh the combined VAT, Income Tax and National Insurance savings provided by a finance lease.

In fact, taking the same facts as in Prianka's case, but assuming instead that the car will be provided to an employee by a VAT-registered higher-rate taxpayer sole trader (or a partnership made up of higher-rate taxpayers), it could take up to 42 years before the savings available under HP exceed those available under a finance lease!

For non-VAT registered businesses acquiring company cars, the considerations are much the same as for a non-VAT registered business acquiring a car for the proprietor's use. However, the fact that there is no balancing adjustment on the sale of the car means that, once again, there will usually be a considerable delay in obtaining full tax relief for the cost of a car purchased under HP.

For cars with CO_2 emissions of more than 75g/km but not exceeding 130g/km, this delay means that a finance lease will usually be preferable.

For cars with CO_2 emissions in excess of 130g/km, the delay in tax relief must be weighed against the 15% reduction in allowable finance lease payments. However, it would usually still take 20 years for the tax relief available under HP to exceed the 85% allowance under a finance lease (based on a car similar to the one acquired by Prianka) – unless the business ceased trading in the meantime.

Based on tax considerations alone, it seems fairly clear that all businesses will nearly always benefit more by holding company cars under finance leases.

'Green' Cars

Businesses purchasing cars with CO_2 emissions of 75g/km or less are eligible for an immediate 100% deduction for the cost of the car (subject to any private use adjustment).

This completely switches the timing of the available tax relief for cars purchased under HP: most of the relief will be available in the year of purchase, rather than the year of sale (or over many years for employee cars).

So, what does this do to the 'lease or buy' question for these cars?

For VAT-registered businesses, finance leases are probably still more beneficial in most cases but, for non-VAT registered businesses, it would generally be more beneficial to buy these cars under HP.

(A balancing charge equal to the sale proceeds, less any applicable private use adjustment, will usually arise on the sale of such a car bought under HP.)

Part 8

Maximising Tax Relief on Borrowings

Chapter 28

How to Maximise Your Interest Tax Deduction

Interest is one of the most important tax deductions for businesses and their owners. The way that we structure our finances can make an enormous difference to the amount we can claim.

The theory behind interest relief is often far more generous than most people realise. In practice, however, keeping track of every potential interest deduction can be a bit of a nightmare. As a result, many business owners do not claim anything like as much as they are theoretically entitled to.

Sole Traders

Interest arises when we borrow money. We can borrow money in many different ways: a mortgage, a bank loan, an overdraft, a credit card or a personal loan.

In principle, it does not matter how we have borrowed the money: whether the interest is tax deductible depends on what we use that money for.

To make life easier, throughout this chapter I will generally refer to any form of borrowing as an 'account'. The interest on any account which is used exclusively for business purposes is fully tax deductible and this is equally true whether we are talking about an overdraft, a credit card or any other form of borrowing.

Hence, if you buy an asset for your business on a credit card and this is the only transaction that you ever make on that card, then all of the interest on that card will be tax deductible.

Using an account for business purposes means buying business assets with the money from that account or otherwise using the account to fund the business – such as by paying staff or rent for the business premises.

The problem is that very few accounts held by sole traders are used exclusively for business purposes. At this point we need to distinguish between a business account with some private use and a private account with some business use. This distinction may sound rather artificial, but it can make a huge difference to the amount of interest relief available.

Business Accounts with Private Use

Many sole traders operate a separate business bank account and some also have a business credit card. These have the advantage of being recognised as business accounts for tax purposes, although the drawback is that you usually have to pay the bank for the privilege in the shape of bank charges, overdraft arrangement fees, etc.

Where these accounts are only ever used for business purposes then all of the interest and other charges on the account are fully deductible.

The problem with most business accounts, however, is that they are also used to pay the proprietor's personal drawings. They may also sometimes be used to meet personal expenses.

Technically, therefore, it should be necessary to track every single transaction going through the account in order to calculate the amount of interest relating to the business transactions.

Thankfully, this mind-boggling level of complexity can usually be avoided as HM Revenue and Customs generally accepts that all of the interest and charges on a business account can be deducted as a business expense.

There is one major proviso, however: the proprietor must not have an overdrawn capital account.

What is a Capital Account?

A proprietor's capital account is a measure of the amount of money which they have put into the business. It is made up of money invested plus profits less drawings and other private expenditure met from business resources. If this measure comes out as a negative figure, they have an overdrawn capital account.

Example

Matt starts up a new business on 1st April 2016. He pays £100,000 to buy business premises, £40,000 for equipment and deposits £10,000 into a business bank account. At this point his capital account stands at £150,000.

In the year ending 31st March 2017, the business makes a profit of £12,000 and Matt draws out £80,000 in cash, as well as using the business bank account to meet private expenditure of £17,000. By this point, the business bank account is overdrawn by £70,000.

Matt's capital account now stands at £65,000 (£150,000 + £12,000 - £80,000 - £17,000). As this is still positive, he may claim a full deduction for all of the overdraft interest on his business bank account.

The profit used to calculate the balance on a proprietor's capital account is the profit before tax. However, where a proprietor's Income Tax liability is paid from a business account, this must be counted as private expenditure.

Many sole traders do not draw up balance sheets for their business, so the capital account exists only in a notional sense. Nevertheless, it still remains an important concept in determining their interest deduction.

Where a balance sheet is prepared for the business, the capital account will appear on it and will be based on general accounting principles. For the purposes of interest deductions, however, the capital account must be adjusted to eliminate any non-cash items included for accounting purposes, such as depreciation and asset revaluations.

Example Continued

In the year ending 31st March 2018, Matt makes a profit of £150,000, draws out £170,000 in cash and uses his business bank account to meet private expenditure of £55,000, including paying his own Income Tax. He also obtains a valuation of £125,000 on his business premises and adopts this new value in his accounts. The business bank account is now overdrawn by £140,000.

Matt's balance sheet now includes a balance of £15,000 on his capital account. This, however, includes the revaluation of £25,000 on his business premises: a non-cash item. Without this, his capital account is £10,000 overdrawn.

Thankfully, however, Matt's accounts also include £16,000 of accumulated depreciation on the equipment he bought in 2016. Adjusting for this non-cash expense, his capital account becomes positive again by £6,000. Once again, therefore, Matt is entitled to claim a full deduction for the interest on his business bank account.

Capital Introduced

As we can see, by using a business bank account Matt has obtained unrestricted tax deductions for his interest costs, even though the account has effectively funded his private expenditure. This is because the capital he introduced into the business plus the profits he has made to date still exceeds the amount of private expenditure and drawings to date.

This is called the 'capital introduced principle' and applies equally to all types of business, including property rental businesses where mortgages over the rental properties are effectively treated the same as business bank accounts.

Overdrawn Capital Accounts

All is not lost if the proprietor's capital account is overdrawn, but things do become a little more complicated since an apportionment of the interest costs becomes necessary.

Example Part 3
By 31st March 2019, Matt's business bank account is overdrawn by £100,000 and his capital account, as adjusted for non-cash items, is overdrawn by £30,000.

This year, Matt will not be entitled to a full deduction for his interest costs and some sort of adjustment will be required. If the bank and capital account balances had been the same all year, he would need to disallow 30% (£30,000/£100,000).

In reality, both balances will have fluctuated over the course of the year, so the apportionment calculation will be more complex than the simple 30% suggested above.

Any reasonable and consistent basis will usually be acceptable. For example, Matt could calculate the apportionment on a month by month basis, using the actual overdraft balance at each month end and assuming that his capital account balance had reduced evenly over the course of the year.

This more detailed calculation will generally be beneficial in a period where the capital account balance is reducing. In Matt's case it would reduce the disallowable proportion of his overdraft interest to around 11.5% instead of the original crude calculation of 30% (assuming that his overdraft was also reducing evenly over the course of the year). To be consistent, however, the same approach would have to be used in a year when the capital account balance was increasing.

Private Accounts with Business Use

If a personal current account were used exclusively for business purposes then any overdraft interest would remain fully allowable. Furthermore, if a business proprietor had two or more personal accounts and used one of them predominantly to run their business, the treatment should be much the same as for a business bank account.

Sometimes, however, a business proprietor will use their only or main personal current account both to run their business and for all of their private expenditure. In this case, it will usually only be possible to claim a deduction for interest costs which can be directly allocated to specific business expenditure. In practice, this is not only horrendously complicated, but may also mean that no deduction is available.

Example Revisited
Let's go back to Matt's first year of trading but assume instead that he ran his business through his own personal bank account. His profits of £12,000 would be paid into that account, but he would have paid out £97,000 for private expenses. Any interest arising must therefore be a personal cost for which no deduction is available.

As we can see, in Matt's case, he was much better off using a business bank account (assuming that his tax relief outweighed the additional charges arising).

The position would be very different, however, if Matt only went into overdraft in order to fund the purchase of business assets or other business expenditure. Here, the position would be similar to that for other personal accounts with some element of business use, such as credit cards or loan accounts.

Two main issues arise: how to allocate the interest charges and how to allocate repayments.

Example 2

On 1ˢᵗ May 2016, Julie has a brought forward balance of £3,000 on her credit card, made up of accumulated interest and private expenditure. She now uses the card to buy equipment for her business costing £4,000. At the end of the month, she is subject to an interest charge of £105. Of this, she can claim a deduction for £60 (£4,000/£7,000 x £105).

Julie makes the minimum repayment of £130 leaving a balance of £6,975 on the card. But what has she repaid?

Clearly, the first part of Julie's repayment covers her interest charge but, after this, she is free to allocate the rest of the repayment as she wishes. To maximise her tax deduction, she therefore allocates it (in her own accounting records) to the private expenditure on the card.

The next month, Julie is subject to an interest charge of £104 and can claim a deduction for £59.64 (£4,000/£6,975 x £104).

Where there are both business and private elements within the same account, the borrower can allocate repayments in the most beneficial way unless there is any agreement with the lender stipulating a different allocation.

By allocating repayments to the private element first, the interest deduction for the business expenditure will be preserved. The payment of the interest itself will generally need to be accounted for first, however, as it is only the capital element of the repayments which can be allocated in this way.

The position is different where the original expenditure was itself for a mixed purpose, as it is not possible to repay only the private element in this case.

Disposals of Business Assets

Where funds have been borrowed to purchase a business asset which is later sold, the interest deduction for those borrowings may continue but this depends on the amount of any disposal proceeds and on what these funds are used for.

Example 2 Continued
In 2018, Julie scraps the equipment which she originally purchased on her credit card and receives disposal proceeds of £50 which she puts into her business bank account. As Julie has kept these proceeds in her business, she can keep claiming a deduction for the interest.

If Julie had kept the disposal proceeds personally, she would have to reduce the business element of her credit card balance by £50 in her interest deduction calculations from that point onwards.

Partnerships

Most of the same principles apply equally to partnerships. Interest on the partnership's business accounts can be claimed in full as long as the partners' capital accounts are not overdrawn.

However, to claim a trading deduction for any interest borne on partners' personal accounts which have been used for business purposes, it is essential that the interest cost is reflected in the partnership accounts.

Alternatively, a partner may make a personal claim for interest on sums borrowed to invest in the partnership, either to purchase a partnership share, lend money to the partnership or purchase equipment for partnership use (including cars). This is known as 'qualifying loan interest' and is deducted from the partner's personal income rather than the partnership profits.

Qualifying loan interest carries the advantage of being deductible from any of the partner's personal income, not just their partnership profits. The disadvantage, however, is that there is no deduction for National Insurance purposes.

Where the interest arises on an account which has also been used for private purposes, the qualifying element is calculated using the same principles which apply when a sole trader uses a private account for business purposes.

However, a loan to buy equipment for use in the partnership generally ceases to be eligible for relief when that equipment is disposed of.

Qualifying loan interest is subject to the annual tax relief 'cap' which is explained in Chapter 50.

Spouses and Civil Partners: Bear It and Grin

Generally speaking, you can only claim a deduction for interest on an account in your own name. You can, however, also claim interest on a joint account with your spouse or civil partner or in their name alone: provided you personally bear the interest cost.

This applies both to sole traders claiming a direct deduction and to partners claiming qualifying loan interest.

Personal Loans

Interest on funds borrowed for business purposes remains tax deductible, regardless of who you borrow it from. Personal loans from friends, family or private investors are subject to the same basic rules as any other form of borrowing.

It is important to ensure that any interest is paid under a formal loan agreement and, where the lender and borrower are connected (e.g. close relatives), the rate of interest charged must not exceed a normal commercial rate. The interest rate can, however, reflect the specific circumstances, such as being unsecured and repayable at any time.

Remember also that the person lending you the money will be subject to Income Tax on the interest that they receive (subject to the personal savings allowance discussed in Chapter 2).

Residential Property Businesses

Note that from 2017/18 onwards owners of residential property businesses will not be able to claim tax relief on their interest and finance costs in the same way that other business owners can.

The new rules will not apply to commercial property or furnished holiday lettings or to properties held inside companies.

Tax relief for interest and finance costs will be phased out over a four-year period commencing in 2017/18, and replaced by a basic rate tax credit as follows:

- 2017/18   75% deducted as normal, 25% at basic rate only
- 2018/19   50% deducted as normal, 50% at basic rate only
- 2019/20   25% deducted as normal, 75% at basic rate only
- 2020/21   All relieved at basic rate only from this year on

Full details of this important tax change are contained in the Taxcafe.co.uk guide *'Landlord Interest'*.

Chapter 29

How to Make Interest on <u>Personal</u> Loans Tax Deductible

The general rule is that interest is a tax deductible expense if the borrowed money is used for business purposes.

It doesn't matter if you use a personal credit card or business overdraft facility to buy that new computer for the business. It also doesn't matter if you borrow against your own home to buy a business property.

In each of these cases the interest on the borrowed money will be tax deductible because the money was used for business purposes.

The fact that the money was borrowed using personal accounts or personal assets is irrelevant.

Example
Harry, a sole trader, buys a new office for £100,000 using a mortgage of £70,000. To fund the deposit, as well as his legal fees and the cost of furnishing the new property, Harry borrows a further £40,000 against his own home.

The extra £40,000 has also been invested in the business, so Harry may also claim interest relief for this element of the mortgage on his home.

If, for example, Harry previously had a mortgage of £80,000 on his home, he will now be able to claim £40,000/£120,000 (one third) of his home's mortgage interest, as well as all the interest on the business property's mortgage.

Harry can make a direct claim for one third of his home's mortgage interest as a direct expense. If he is also making a 'use of home' claim (see Chapter 3) he should only include the remaining two thirds of his home's mortgage interest in that calculation.

Finally, please note that not all money borrowed for business purposes is fully tax deductible. Residential property businesses will have the tax relief on their interest and other finance costs gradually reduced from April 2017 onwards.

Part 9

Business Property

Chapter 30

Business Premises:
Rent or Buy?

Is it better to rent or buy your business premises? There are both tax and non-tax issues to consider:

Tax Relief

Rent paid for business premises is generally fully tax deductible, whatever type of business you have.

The same goes for interest paid on any mortgage, or other loan, to buy business property.

Most of the actual purchase price of the property itself, however, will not usually attract any tax relief – with capital allowances only available on some of the fixtures, fittings and equipment within the property (see Chapter 32).

Note too that tax relief for interest paid by residential property businesses will be restricted from 2017/18 onwards. So if you take out a loan to buy a commercial property, out of which you run your residential property letting business, the tax relief on your interest payments will be restricted.

Capital Gains Tax

If you buy your own trading premises, you may qualify for several Capital Gains Tax reliefs that other property investors do not enjoy. Note the word 'trading'. This means investment businesses (e.g. property investment businesses) do not generally qualify.

Rollover relief allows you to roll over your capital gains into the purchase of new trading property. You can buy the new property between a year before and three years after selling the original property.

This effectively defers any Capital Gains Tax liability on the original property until the new property is sold and gives your business flexibility to change premises and grow without adverse tax consequences.

All of the old property's sale proceeds must be reinvested. Any shortfall is deducted from the amount of gain eligible for rollover. Relief is also restricted if there is less than full trading use of the property.

Entrepreneurs' Relief

Entrepreneurs' Relief allows individuals to pay Capital Gains Tax at just 10% when they sell their business premises, but generally only if they sell their business as well.

Remember, however, if you sell your premises without selling your business, you may not have to pay Capital Gains Tax immediately, as you can defer the gain using rollover relief.

Entrepreneurs' Relief may also be available where a business partner personally owns the partnership's trading premises. Relief is restricted where rent is paid for the use of the property after April 2008 however.

Entrepreneurs' Relief is subject to a generous lifetime limit of £10 million of capital gains per person.

Property Pensions

Commercial property is one type of direct bricks and mortar property investment you can put inside your self-invested personal pension (SIPP).

Investing via a SIPP allows a higher-rate taxpayer to effectively buy property at a 40% discount, paid for by the taxman, as well as completely avoiding both Income Tax and Capital Gains Tax.

The problem with SIPPs is the severe borrowing restriction – generally no more than 50% of net assets. Even if you have £100,000 sitting in your SIPP account, you can only borrow an extra £50,000. Not many commercial properties come that cheap.

Nevertheless, for those with large pension savings, who can afford to make big pension contributions, or can team up with business associates, this is still a viable option.

In summary, buying your own trading premises could produce additional tax benefits not enjoyed by other property investors.

Non-Tax Benefits & Drawbacks

When you buy business premises using a mortgage, you are generally swapping rent for interest. Effectively the bank becomes your landlord! These are the pros and cons:

- Depending on the level of interest rates, property prices and rental values, one route will always be cheaper than the other and the disparity will change over time. Every property is different.

- If you rent you will never be exposed to falling property values... and likewise you will never benefit from rising property prices.

- Rents can be more predictable than interest payments and can be agreed many years into the future. Interest payments can be fixed but not usually for long periods.

- A long lease agreement could bind your business and harm its growth.

- Tenants do not enjoy the same security as owners – they have no control over the long-term location of their businesses.

- You continue to be liable for rental payments under a lease even if you cease trading. If you own the property, you could sell it, although this process can take time.

Chapter 31

Repairs Save More Tax than Improvements

Repairs expenditure is generally eligible for immediate and full Income Tax relief.

Capital improvement expenditure, on the other hand, does not usually qualify for Income Tax relief and this is where the greatest area of difficulty lies: knowing the difference between a repair and an improvement. It can make a huge difference to your business's tax bill.

Example
Gwen has an old office block with a damaged wall. If Gwen spends £50,000 to have the wall repaired, she will be able to claim tax relief for this expenditure. If she has the wall demolished and has an extension built for £100,000, she will get no tax relief at all.

No relief is allowed for the notional cost of repair work which would otherwise have been needed if the improvement had not taken place.

(Note that, in this chapter, when I say 'no relief', I am talking about Income Tax relief. Most improvement expenditure will be an eligible deduction for Capital Gains Tax purposes on a sale of the property.)

What is a Capital Improvement?

Judging whether something is an improvement is not a question of aesthetics or taste. Whenever you add something 'extra' to an asset which wasn't there before, you've made a capital improvement and it means you cannot deduct the cost as a repair expense. If you built a new extension on the side of a Victorian building, it would be an 'improvement' for tax purposes – whatever Prince Charles might think!

Alterations will generally also be capital improvements, even if nothing is actually added. If you demolish a wall to combine two rooms into one, you will not have added anything, but it will still be a capital improvement.

Like For Like

Replacing 'like for like' will generally be a repair, unless:

- You replace an asset in its entirety, or

- The replacement is of a significantly higher standard

Each building and all its fixtures is generally regarded as a single asset for this purpose. Moveable items like machinery or furniture are separate assets.

For example, let us suppose you have a property with a separate garage at the rear. If you demolish the garage and replace it, this will be a capital improvement and no relief will be available. This is because the garage is a separate, stand-alone, asset and replacing it therefore constitutes capital expenditure.

Contrast this with replacing a staircase. As long as there is no improvement element to the expenditure, this would be allowable as a repair because the staircase is not a separate asset in its own right. If you widened the staircase at the same time, however, this would then be a capital improvement.

Where the replacement is of a higher standard, this will generally be regarded as a capital improvement. For example, replacing a porcelain bath with a marble one would be capital expenditure.

However, where the replacement is simply the modern equivalent of the original item, this is not regarded as an improvement and can be claimed as a 'like for like' repair. The best example of this is replacing single-glazed windows with standard double-glazed units and HMRC has specifically confirmed that this is accepted as a repair.

Integral Features

Certain items within commercial property are classed as 'integral features', including electrical systems, plumbing, heating, air conditioning, lifts and escalators. The good news is that these items qualify for capital allowances (see Chapter 32).

On the downside, however, expenditure on replacing part of an integral feature is classed as a capital improvement if such expenditure amounts to more than half of the cost of replacing the entire feature within any twelve month period.

Where significant repairs are taking place, it may therefore be worth staggering them over a longer period in order to avoid this problem.

New Properties

Generally speaking, any expenditure which restores an asset to its original condition will be regarded as a repair. When I say 'original condition' though, I am talking about the condition of the asset when you acquired it.

If you buy a property with a hole in the roof, the cost of repairing that roof will be capital expenditure because you are improving on the condition of the property when you bought it.

In practice, normal repairs and redecoration work on newly acquired properties is usually considered allowable. Such expenditure will generally be regarded as 'normal' if the work required is unlikely to have had any significant impact on the property's purchase price (or rent payable in the case of a leased property).

For example, let's suppose you buy new office premises. The property could be occupied as it stands, but is really in need of redecoration. The cost of this redecoration work should usually be allowed as a deduction against your business profits.

If the property is severely dilapidated beyond normal 'wear and tear' however, the work may be so extensive that it has to be treated as a capital improvement.

In some borderline cases, it may be worth considering occupying the property first in order to ensure that the expenditure can be properly regarded as a repair.

Example
Owen buys an office that hasn't been decorated since the 1970s. He carries out some work to ensure the property meets the necessary health and safety standards (this work will be a capital improvement) and then occupies it for a year. After that, he has the whole place redecorated. The cost of the redecoration should now be an allowable deduction.

This approach will not help in extreme cases (like a hole in the roof), but could be worth considering where there is extensive redecoration work to be carried out.

Collateral Damage

Where repairs are merely incidental to a capital improvement, the cost will all be regarded as capital expenditure. For example, you might have an extension built and then need to redecorate the adjacent room – this will all be capital.

If, however, you can put up with the slightly damaged decor in that adjacent room for a while, redecorating it later, in say a year or two, should usually be allowed as a repair.

Splitting the Cost

Although you cannot claim for repair work which is merely incidental to a capital improvement, you can claim the repair element of any work which has both repairs and improvement elements.

This is particularly common where a kitchen or bathroom is replaced. All the 'like for like' replacements of units, worktops, sinks, etc, can be claimed as a repair. Only additional or higher standard items need to be treated as capital improvements. Incidental decorating work can be apportioned between the repairs and improvements on any reasonable basis.

Remember here that 'higher standard' doesn't mean just more modern. If the only 'improvement' is a more modern material, it's still a repair.

Splitting out your expenditure on an 'item by item' basis can yield significant benefits in the shape of deductible repairs expenditure. In this way, you can improve your property and still get your tax relief.

Chapter 32

Integral Features: Claiming Tax Relief on the Purchase Price

Thanks to the annual investment allowance, most businesses buying commercial property are currently entitled to an immediate tax deduction of up to £200,000 (a higher allowance is available if your accounting period straddles 1st January 2016 – see Chapter 16).

For many years, there was an ongoing battle to define the boundary between buildings, which do not usually qualify for any capital allowances, and the equipment within the buildings, which does qualify.

The category of 'integral features' introduced in 2008 covers the borderline items and provides tax relief for millions of pounds of commercial property expenditure. The items qualifying for tax relief include:

- Electrical lighting and power systems
- Cold water systems
- Space or water heating systems, air conditioning, ventilation and air purification systems and floors or ceilings comprised in such systems
- Lifts, escalators and moving walkways
- External solar shading

In a nutshell: All the wiring, lighting, plumbing, heating and air conditioning in any commercial property qualifies for capital allowances, with immediate 100% tax relief for up to £200,000 spent on these items (a higher allowance is available this year if your accounting period straddles 1st January 2016).

Almost any type of commercial property will qualify, including shops, offices, hotels, doctors' and dentists' surgeries, workshops and garages.

To qualify for capital allowances, the property needs to be used in a qualifying business, but not necessarily by the owner. This means that many commercial property landlords also qualify for relief.

The property does not need to be newly built – the integral features regime applies to any property purchased after 5th April 2008.

For property purchases taking place after 5th April 2012, the purchaser and seller now generally have to agree a value for the qualifying fixtures within the property and make a joint election to that effect (known as a 'Section 198 Election'), which the purchaser has to submit to HM Revenue and Customs within a fixed time period after the purchase in support of their claim.

For purchases taking place after 5th April 2014, the purchaser will not generally be able to claim capital allowances on any fixtures where the seller would have been entitled to make a capital allowances claim, but failed to do so. Such failures to make legitimate claims are commonplace, so it is vital to check the seller's capital allowances claims history.

This does not, however, include cases where the seller was unable to make a claim: such as where they had bought the property before April 2008 and were unable to claim capital allowances on some of the integral features.

For further details see the Taxcafe.co.uk guide *How to Save Property Tax*.

Qualifying expenditure in excess of the annual investment allowance generally attracts writing down allowances at 18%, although the rate for 'integral features' is just 8%.

This rather measly rate of 8% can sometimes be avoided by simply allocating the annual investment allowance to 'integral features' in preference to other qualifying expenditure.

Subject to the procedures for second-hand property discussed above, people buying commercial property will often be able to benefit from significant tax savings by allocating part of the purchase price to 'integral features' and other items of qualifying equipment within the property, such as white goods, sanitary ware and moveable partitioning.

More than 30% of the price of a modern office could often qualify for allowances and even an empty retail unit could yield a claim of around 15%.

Purchase price allocations must be made on a reasonable basis and a surveyor can help you with this. Make sure you get a surveyor who knows about integral features though!

Where you are required to agree a value for qualifying items with the seller of the property, this will usually only bind you in respect of items on which they either have, or could have, made a capital allowances claim. If they held the property before April 2008, this will not generally include any cold water plumbing or electrical systems, so you will still be free to claim allowances on these.

If you want to replace any of the 'integral features' within a property (e.g. rewiring it, or putting in a new heating system) you can claim tax relief on that expenditure too: in addition to any tax relief claimed on the original integral features that you rip out.

It is important to ensure that the original integral features are used (i.e. the building is occupied) for some period before they are replaced.

Chapter 33

Loan Arrangement Fees

From time to time most business owners consider re-financing: either to move to a fixed-rate loan or just to get a better deal.

But, as we all know, re-financing does not come cheap. Apart from interest on the new loan, there are always those 'extra' costs to be considered: loan arrangement fees, mortgage broker's fees, penalty fees on the redemption of the old loan and perhaps some legal fees or survey fees in the case of mortgages and other secured loans.

Loan arrangement fees are often all too easily forgotten as they are usually added to the new loan balance (often costing twice as much in the long run due to the interest charged as a result).

But these are a real cost and, where the loan has been taken out for business purposes, they can and should be deducted from business profits.

The loan arrangement fees, together with any other costs incurred as a result of the re-financing, are classed as 'incidental costs of raising loan finance' (let's call them 'loan finance costs' for short).

Generally accepted accounting practice states that these costs should be written off against business profits over the life of the loan and this is one of those cases where tax law follows the same principles.

Example

Jack is a sole trader running a small shop in Cardiff. He has an existing mortgage over the shop with Useless Bank plc. Jack decides to move his mortgage to Slightlybetter Bank plc. He incurs broker's fees of £500, legal fees of £400 and a loan arrangement fee of £2,000 which is added to the new mortgage. The new mortgage is for a ten year period.

Jack has incurred a total of £2,900 of loan finance costs and can therefore claim £290 as a deduction against his trading profits in each of the next ten years. The fact that the loan arrangement fees were added to his mortgage makes no difference to this.

Accelerating Relief

Spreading these costs over the life of the loan is based on accounting practice rather than tax law. We can therefore look to accounting practice to provide some possible means to accelerate relief for these costs.

Firstly: materiality. Accounting practice does not require absolute precision but only requires that accounts are not materially misstated. Hence, where the loan finance costs are very small in comparison to the total size of the business, it would be reasonable to deduct the whole cost in the period that the loan is taken out.

Secondly, where a cost has been incurred but has outlived its usefulness, it is appropriate to write off any remaining balance. Hence, if Jack were to re-finance his shop again after a few years, any remaining part of the original £2,900 costs in the example which had not yet been claimed could then be deducted in full.

Taking this a step further, it is worth considering the fact that the modern trend is to re-finance loans at fairly frequent intervals, every few years.

Where the business has a strategy of refinancing at frequent intervals, say every five years, it is reasonable for it to deduct its loan finance costs over this period, rather than the whole term of the loan. In Jack's case, this would give him a deduction of £580 each year for five years instead of £290 each year for ten.

Penalty Fees

As we all know, banks don't let go so easily and will usually charge a penalty for the early repayment of the old loan.

If a company or partnership incurs such a cost it can be treated as a business cost and a full deduction can be claimed straight away.

For sole traders, HMRC takes the view that such costs are a personal cost and hence not allowable. We regard this view as fundamentally flawed and would argue that, if re-financing has been carried out for sound business reasons, the costs arising should be deducted from business profits.

Saving money is a pretty sound business reason, so a lot of re-financing carried out by business owners would meet our criterion!

It is important to note that HMRC's view on this issue is simply that: a view. It is not the law. Where the law itself (set by Parliament and the Courts) states that something is not allowable, there is no argument!

Other Qualifying Loans

Sole traders, partnerships and companies carrying out re-financing should all be able to claim the costs incurred under the principles set out above. This would include a sole trader who re-mortgaged their own home to invest funds in their business or to replace a mortgage previously used for the same purpose.

Directors, shareholders and business partners who borrow money to invest in, or lend to, a company or a trading partnership are generally able to claim tax relief for their interest costs. This is known as 'qualifying loan interest'. Sadly, this relief does not extend to loan finance costs. It is worth bearing this in mind when weighing up the comparative merits of different mortgage deals.

Buying New Properties

When you buy a new property, most of the incidental costs arising (Stamp Duty Land Tax, legal fees, etc) have to be treated as part of the capital cost of the property.

Where the purchase is financed with a mortgage, however, part of the legal fees you incur will relate to arranging the loan (dealing with the charge over the property, etc.).

When the property is a business property, you should therefore arrange for the lawyer to charge the costs relating to the mortgage separately. These can then be claimed against your business profits over the life of the loan.

This also applies to other costs incurred specifically in order to obtain the mortgage, such as extra survey fees for example.

Residential Property Businesses

Note that from 2017/18 onwards owners of residential property businesses will not be able to claim tax relief on their interest and finance costs in the same way that other business owners can.

The restriction will also apply to loan arrangement fees and other finance costs.

For more information see the Taxcafe.co.uk guide *'Landlord Interest'*.

Part 10

E-Commerce

Chapter 34

Websites, Domain Names and Other Internet Costs

Thousands of UK businesses sell their wares on eBay and Amazon.

Over 70% of UK adults now shop online. A total of £114 billion in online retail sales took place in 2015 – an 11% increase over the year before.

What about the tax treatment of businesses involved in e-commerce? There aren't any specific e-commerce tax laws as such, but there are a number of tax rules and tax saving strategies that apply more to this type of business than others.

Website Costs

These days you can make a living online even if you don't have a website. Selling on eBay is an obvious example but other sites like Amazon also let you set up your own store and sell your wares to their many thousands of customers. There are no set up costs involved.

If you do want a website for your business, is the cost of developing it tax deductible?

Unfortunately, the position here is far from clear, as this is a new and developing area of tax law. However, the general rule is that expenditure which creates an asset with 'enduring benefit' should be treated as capital expenditure. 'Enduring benefit' is generally taken to mean something with a useful life of more than two years.

Where you have a simple website used solely to advertise or promote your business, it should be acceptable to simply claim the development costs as they arise on the basis that the site has no 'enduring benefit'. Current accounting principles would support this view.

But, where the website is a fully functioning e-commerce store that directly generates income, you will generally need to treat it as a capital asset and the development costs will therefore be capital expenditure.

Capital costs normally have to be written off for tax purposes over many years BUT these days, thanks to the annual investment allowance, a lot of capital expenditure is fully tax deductible in year one anyway.

Hence, despite the uncertainty surrounding this issue, most businesses should still be able to claim an immediate tax deduction for their website development costs.

When Capital Spending is High

Those businesses that have to be careful are the ones developing fully functioning e-commerce websites (capital expenditure) that have already exceeded the annual investment allowance.

The annual investment allowance is currently £200,000 per year (more if your current accounting period straddles 1st January 2016) and is generous enough in most cases.

However, there could also be instances where your business's combined spending on vans, computers, equipment, integral features in buildings, etc, exceeds the annual investment allowance limit for the relevant period.

If you then spend more money developing an e-commerce website, the cost will only qualify for capital allowances of 18% per year.

This could prove costly if you plan on spending a lot of money developing the website – a website that simply promotes your business will probably only cost a few hundred pounds; a sophisticated e-commerce website could cost thousands.

Maintaining and Updating a Website

Once your website is up and running, the cost of maintaining and updating it (e.g. changing prices), including web hosting costs, should be classed as revenue spending and will be fully tax deductible.

Domain Names

It costs around £10 a year to register or renew a website domain name. This cost is generally tax deductible.

Where it gets more complicated is when you spend a significant amount of money buying a domain name that someone else has already registered: like the $36 million paid for insurance.com!

Whereas websites are treated as tangible assets for tax purposes, like computer software, and therefore qualify for capital allowances, the cost of buying a domain name is treated as an intangible asset.

Sadly, for self-employed business owners, there is no tax relief on the cost of intangible assets.

Advertising

If you want to advertise your business online using Google Adwords or some other website then, like most advertising costs, the cost is usually fully tax deductible.

Transaction Costs & Commissions

When you sell online, you will inevitably incur a variety of charges: credit card transaction fees, commissions to resellers, product listing fees, etc. All of these costs are deductible when calculating the taxable profits of your business.

However, sometimes these costs are a bit opaque – there is no invoice as such to pay, the costs are simply deducted from your account. It is therefore important to calculate these costs and give the details to your accountant when your business tax return is being completed, so that your taxable profits are not overstated.

Buying Online

Even if your business doesn't sell online, there are lots of things you may want to buy online: computers, stationery, office supplies, etc. You can save hundreds if not thousands of pounds by shopping online.

Sometimes you may wish to make these purchases using a credit card but if you are a small business owner you may not have a business credit card.

In that case a solution is to use your own personal credit card – preferably a dedicated one that you set aside for business purchases. You can set up a direct debit linked to the business bank account to clear the balance each month.

There are lots of great deals for business owners on eBay. To buy items here one solution is to set up a dedicated Paypal account for the business. Paypal charges relating to business purchases are tax deductible.

Some eBay sellers are VAT registered businesses, although they often do not advertise that fact or issue proper invoices because most of their customers are private individuals. Make sure you ask for a VAT invoice so you can reclaim the tax if you are VAT registered.

Chapter 35

Tax Saving Opportunities for Internet Businesses

If you are starting a new dedicated internet business, you may be able to take advantage of the following tax-saving opportunities:

Working from Home

A major shackle for many new businesses is having to rent a shop or office to attract customers. This means overheads – rent to a landlord and possibly business rates to the local council. These have to be covered each month before you make a penny of profit.

However, if your business is wholly based on e-commerce, you may be able to work from home. The great thing about working from home is that, instead of incurring new premises costs, you can reduce your existing ones!

For example, let's say you use a room in your house as your office. If the house has five rooms in total (ignoring the kitchen, hallways and bathrooms), this means you could potentially claim up to one fifth of all your household costs for tax purposes

Costs that can be claimed include: mortgage interest, council tax, repairs, insurance, electricity, gas and cleaning. (See Chapter 3 for more information.)

Part-time Businesses

Possibly the best way to start any business is part time. Having a back-up income significantly reduces the risk and gives you breathing space to get things up and running. Many internet businesses are run permanently on a part-time basis to provide a second source of income.

The tax treatment of part-time businesses is much the same as for any business. Providing it is a genuine business, you should be able to claim all of your expenses as normal, although some of these would have to be reduced to reflect the part-time nature of the business: e.g. your home office tax deduction.

If your part-time business makes a loss in the early stages you can offset this against your other income (e.g. salary income) and capital gains. However, you would have to be able to prove that you are in business with the intention of making a profit.

Loss relief for part-timers is restricted to a maximum of £25,000 per tax year if you spend less than 10 hours per week working in the business.

This type of loss relief is not available if you run your business through a limited company because company losses cannot be offset against the owner's personal income.

Further restrictions in this type of loss relief for sole traders and business partners are now in force as part of the tax relief 'cap' explained in Chapter 50.

Living Abroad

The great thing about many internet businesses is they can be run from anywhere. So, if you fancy a complete lifestyle change you could move abroad and set up your internet business in another country.

There are many countries that have no or very low Income Tax and Corporation Tax. Brits have to work 154 days per year just to pay their taxes, so it's easy to see why some consider moving abroad to save tax.

Part 11

Year-End Tax Planning & Pro-active Accounting

Chapter 36

Year-End Tax Planning Strategies

In this chapter we will take a look at a variety of year-end tax planning strategies.

By deferring income for just one day, it may be possible to postpone tax for a whole year; by accelerating expenses, it is often possible to enjoy tax relief one year earlier.

Year-end tax planning is even more powerful if you expect your tax rate to fall for the next year: you will not only be postponing tax, you will be saving it as well.

Business Year-End Planning

For business owners, there are effectively two types of year-end planning to be considered.

Firstly, there's personal year-end planning: things like making pension contributions or investing in tax shelters like venture capital trusts. The tax year end on 5th April is the key date for this type of planning.

In this chapter, however, we are going to focus on business year-end planning: *where your own accounting date is the key date.*

For example, a sole trader with a 31st March accounting date needs to take action by 31st March 2017 to save tax for 2016/17; a sole trader with a 30th April accounting date has until 30th April 2017 to take action which will usually save them tax for 2017/18.

Business year-end tax planning should generally only be about accelerating the expenditure that you need to make anyway: it's seldom worth spending extra money just to save tax.

Accelerating Expenses

Any liabilities incurred by your accounting date can reduce your taxable profits, even if you only pay the bill later.

In a few instances, where there is a legal obligation to have work carried out, just getting a quote by your accounting date may be enough – repairs required to get an M.O.T. certificate on a van would be a good example.

An easy way to reduce your tax bill is to buy large items which enjoy an immediate 100% deduction under the annual investment allowance. Examples include vans, computers and office equipment. Integral features in commercial property also qualify, including wiring, lighting, plumbing, heating and air-conditioning.

Cars

Cars are another item that can help business owners cut their tax bills. You can currently claim up to 18% of the cost as a tax deduction in the accounting year that you purchase the car (8% if the car has higher CO_2 emissions).

For self-employed business owners, the allowance is restricted to reflect private use, but even just one quarter business use of a £25,000 car could give you a deduction of £1,125.

New cars with CO_2 emissions of 75g/km or less are currently eligible for an immediate 100% enhanced capital allowance.

If you are selling a car, you will also often benefit by completing the transaction before your accounting date. Sales of cars often give rise to balancing allowances which can sometimes significantly reduce your taxable profits. (Beware, however, that balancing charges can also sometimes arise: so do your sums first.)

Business Property

If you own your own business premises, one of the best ways to save tax is to carry out repairs before your accounting date.

Anything classed as an improvement is no help, however, as tax relief on this expenditure is only provided when the property is sold (except 'integral features' which attract capital allowances).

Some types of property expenditure are often classed as repairs for tax purposes BUT may increase the value of your property: such as new (replacement) kitchens or bathrooms, double glazing, re-wiring and decorating.

Many property owners think of these items as improvements, but they are often fully tax deductible repairs, providing you follow the rules. (See Chapter 31 for more information.)

Deferring Income

For businesses supplying goods, it makes sense to consider delaying the completion of sales until after the accounting date, so that the profit falls into the next period. Commercial pressures will often dictate the opposite, however!

Sadly, for businesses supplying services, deferring income is not so easy. A few years ago, these businesses could defer income just by delaying issuing invoices. Unfortunately, you are now generally required to include all of the income which has effectively been earned by the accounting date, whether invoiced or not.

However, where commercial pressures allow, you could still consider putting off some work until after your year end, so that the income 'earned' by that date is less. Most people would agree that two half-finished jobs are worth less than one completed one.

Change Your Accounting Date

One of the most radical year-end tax planning strategies you can adopt is to change the year-end itself! Most businesses are free to change their accounting date at least once every six years. (See Chapter 37 for more information.)

Year-end Planning in Reverse

If you expect to be paying tax at a higher rate in the next tax year, it may be better to do the complete opposite: accelerate your income and defer your expenses.

Those who may wish to consider reversing their year-end tax planning in this way include individuals expecting their marginal tax rate to rise from 29% to 42%; from 42% to 47%; or from 42% to 62%.

How to Accelerate Income and Defer Expenses

If you expect your tax rate to rise next year, you may wish to consider accelerating income or deferring expenses in order to bring more taxable income into the current year. Some of the techniques you could consider include:

- Defer capital expenditure in order to claim the annual investment allowance next year instead of this year.

- Defer gift aid and pension contributions to after 5th April.

- Complete orders and projects and bring billing up to date. Accounting rules often require part-completed work to be brought into account, but there is still a large element of profit dependent on completion and billing in many cases. For example, two half completed projects are, in accounting terms, likely to yield less profit than a single completed project of the same size.

- Connected businesses (e.g. wife has business, husband also has his own business): make extra sales to connected businesses in advance of year end.

Chapter 37

Change Your Accounting Date

We looked at year-end tax planning for businesses in Chapter 36. Another thing you may be able to do is change the year-end itself!

Most businesses are free to change their accounting date at least once every six years. This means they will either be shortening an accounting period, or extending it. The maximum permitted length for an accounting period is generally eighteen months.

Sole Traders

It's easier for sole traders to change their accounting date than it is for companies because they don't need to tell Companies House. The consequences of the change can be much more complex, however – but extremely beneficial in some cases.

The sole trader simply draws up accounts to their new accounting date and puts this date on their Tax Return.

For the new date to be effective for tax purposes:

- The Tax Return must be submitted on time,
- The new accounting period must not exceed 18 months, and
- Unless the change is made for *commercial* (non-tax) reasons, there must not have been another earlier change in the previous five tax years.

Short Accounting Period

If you've shortened your accounting period, you will have either one or two accounting dates falling in the tax year. Remember the tax year runs from 6th April one year to 5th April the next year.

If just one accounting date falls in the tax year, you will be taxed on your profits for the period of twelve months ending on your new accounting date.

This means that part of your profits for the previous accounting period will be taxed twice. Any profit which is taxed twice is known as an 'overlap profit'. This also frequently occurs when you start a new business.

Relief for your 'overlap profit' is given when you cease trading, or sometimes on a subsequent change of accounting date. We'll come on to that in a minute.

It may seem like a bad idea to be taxed on the same profit twice, but sometimes you can generate future overlap relief, which could later save you tax at 42% or even more, without paying any extra tax now.

Example
Matt draws up accounts to 31st March.

His profits for the year ended 31st March 2016 were £18,000. His profits for the rest of 2016 fell to just £300 per month.

Matt decides to shorten his accounting period and prepares accounts for the nine months ended 31st December 2016.

Because just one accounting date (31st December 2016) will fall into the 2016/17 tax year, Matt will have to pay tax on his profits for the 12 month period to 31st December 2016.

This means his profits for January to March 2016 will be subject to tax twice – once when he submits his accounts to 31st March 2016 and again when he submits his accounts to 31st December 2016.

However, because his profits to 31st December 2016 are so low, there is no tax to pay. His taxable profits are:

Three months to 31st March 2016: 3/12 x £18,000 = £4,500
Nine months to 31st December 2016: 9 x £300 = £2,700

Total: £7,200

This is less than both the personal allowance and the National Insurance earnings threshold. Matt has thus created an overlap of £4,500 available for future use with no current tax cost. If he's a higher rate taxpayer when he ceases trading, this could save him £1,890 (£4,500 x 42%).

If two accounting dates fall in the year, you will be taxed on the profits of both periods. This means you are taxed on more than twelve months of profit in one year, but it also means you may be eligible to claim overlap relief: more on that later.

Long Accounting Periods

If you extend your accounting period, you will either have one accounting date falling in the tax year or none. Where no accounting date falls in the current tax year, you will effectively be taxed on the same twelve months' worth of profit both this year and next year, calculated on a time-apportionment basis.

Example
Noel draws up accounts for the fifteen months ended 30th June 2016 showing a profit of £15,000. As no accounting date falls into 2015/16, he is taxed on a profit of £12,000 (£15,000 x 12/15).

Noel is taxed on the same sum in 2016/17, thus creating an 'overlap profit' of £9,000 (2 x £12,000 - £15,000).

Unlike Matt, Noel's overlap profit comes at a price: basic rate tax and National Insurance totalling £635 in 2015/16 and £555 in 2016/17. But Noel would probably have paid similar amounts anyway.

Furthermore, he has the benefit that tax on profits arising between July and March will now always be deferred by a year and he has potential overlap relief worth £3,780 (£9,000 x 42%), or even more, to claim in the future.

Using Overlap Relief Now

If you extend your accounting period but your new accounting date still falls in the same tax year, you are taxed on the profits of the whole period. As this is more than twelve months, you can claim relief for some or all of any overlap profit which arose in the past.

Most people whose existing accounting date is not 31st March or 5th April will have overlap profits from when they started trading or from when the self-assessment system began in 1997. You can find your overlap profit in Box 70 on the (full) self-employment pages of your tax return. If there's nothing there check with your accountant: many of them neglect to complete this box as it only affects future periods.

The overlap relief available on a change of accounting date is based on the length of the extended accounting period in excess of twelve months as a proportion of the original period of overlap (but the relief cannot exceed the total amount of overlap profit available).

This means that extending your accounting period to a date falling later in the same tax year will be beneficial whenever your profits have fallen below their original level at the time that the overlap was created.

Example

Catherine has overlap profits brought forward of £36,000 due to a previous overlap period of nine months. She therefore has overlap profits of £4,000 per month.

Her profits have now fallen to just £2,000 per month, so Catherine decides to draw up accounts for the eighteen months ended 31st October 2016. Her taxable profit for 2016/17 is:

Profit for period ended 31/10/2016: 18 x £2,000	*£36,000*
Less overlap relief for period in excess of 12 months	
6/9 x £36,000	*£24,000*

Taxable profit:	*£12,000*
	=======

If Catherine had stuck to her usual accounting date, her taxable profit would have been £24,000 (12 x £2,000). The change of accounting date has halved her taxable profit, saving her £3,480 in Income Tax (at 20%) and National Insurance (at 9%).

The only drawback here is that Catherine has effectively 'cashed in' some of her overlap relief at an effective rate of just 29%. This could be disadvantageous if her marginal tax rate is higher when she eventually ceases trading. On the other hand, that could be many years away and inflation may have severely eroded the value of her overlap profits by then: a bird in the hand is worth two in the bush!

Partnerships

Partnerships can generally change their accounting date in much the same way as sole traders.

The impact on each partner will differ, however, as each will have their own individual overlap profit and marginal tax rate. The same change of accounting date could be beneficial for one partner, but disastrous for another.

Limited Liability Partnerships which change their accounting date need to advise Companies House using form LL AA01 and are subject to the same deadlines as a company.

Chapter 38

Cost of Sales

The biggest deduction in most business accounts is cost of sales.

Unfortunately, that deduction is itself also subject to a deduction: closing stock and work-in-progress.

A deduction from a deduction means an increase in taxable profits and we can save tax by reducing it as much as possible.

Closing stock is a measure of the value of goods still on hand or services not yet completed at the accounting date.

The treatment of goods and services differs a little. In this chapter, we are going to look at goods: tangible products which the business sells.

Closing stock needs to be valued at the lower of cost or 'net realisable value'. Let's look at cost first.

Direct Costs Only

The stock figure in your accounts only needs to include the direct costs of acquiring or producing your product, so the first thing to do is to look at your costing system and make sure that you're not including any indirect costs.

You do, however, need to include production overheads, such as factory or workshop electricity costs and business rates. The electricity or business rates for an office would, however, usually be an indirect cost and should generally be excluded.

Net Realisable Value

Let's say it has cost you £100 to make a product and you would normally sell it for £120. However, to sell the product, you will need to incur advertising and other costs of £10. This still leaves you a profit so you would continue to value the stock of this product at £100.

Let's suppose, however, that a competitor launches a better product, so you can only sell yours for £105 and your advertising and other selling costs increase to £25. The product now has a net realisable value of £80 (£105 - £25).

In effect, you know that you are now going to make a loss on this product. You are allowed to anticipate this loss by reducing your stock value in your accounts to just £80. This will effectively give you tax relief of £20 per item now, even before you sell the product.

It is very often worth having a good look at your stock to see which items can be valued at less than cost in order to provide tax relief for your effective loss now. Things to look out for include:

- Old or damaged goods which are no longer usable

- Obsolete stock superseded by changes in fashion or technology

- Surplus stock for which there is no demand

- Missing items (perhaps lost or stolen)

It's Only a Matter of Time

Before you get your whole workforce out checking stock, it is worth reflecting that stock valuations generally only create a timing difference.

When you sell the items in stock, their accounts value will form a deduction from your sale proceeds. If you reduce your stock value in this year's accounts, you will generally have a bigger taxable profit next year as a result.

Hence, although the savings yielded by reducing stock value can be worthwhile, they are often only temporary.

The position is different, however, if you anticipate having a lower tax rate next year than this year, such as when your profits are expected to fall below the higher-rate tax threshold (£43,000 for 2016/17; £45,000 for 2017/18 – except for Scottish taxpayers: see Chapter 2). In these cases, getting relief for the fall in the value of your stock this year will actually yield a permanent saving.

On the other hand, if you're expecting an *increase* in profits next year, with a higher tax rate as a result, any reduction in the value of your stock in this year's accounts could give rise to an overall tax cost. You still need to apply the same principles to valuing your stock but you might want to take a more optimistic (but reasonable) view of its net realisable value.

Chapter 39

Bad Debts

There's only one good thing about a bad debt: tax relief.

But when is a debt 'bad' and how do you get the most out of the available relief?

Write-offs and Provisions

Bad debt relief generally follows accounting treatment. Where a debt is written off, or a specific accounting provision is made against it, tax relief should usually follow. (Special rules apply to debts between connected parties, e.g. a husband and wife.)

A debt is 'written off' if it is simply removed from the books of the business altogether: i.e. you've given up all hope of recovering it.

A 'bad debt provision' is slightly different. This is an accounting adjustment which you make to reflect the possibility of not getting paid, but the debt itself stays on the books whilst you continue to pursue it.

"That sounds great", you may be saying, "I'll make a provision against all my debts and get tax relief for the lot!"

Sadly, this would not work. Accounting principles only permit you to make a bad debt provision where there is genuine doubt over the recovery of the debt. If your accounts don't follow generally accepted principles, tax relief would be denied.

However, you can still accelerate relief for bad debts when your accounts are being prepared.

Example
At 30th June 2016, Toshiko is owed £10,000 by Victim Limited, a good customer for many years. By the end of August, Victim Limited has paid all but £2,500 of this sum.

At this point, however, Greedybank plc refuses to renew Victim Limited's overdraft facility and the company is forced into liquidation.

In September, Toshiko is preparing her accounts for the year ended 30th June 2016. It is unclear whether any further sums will be received from Victim Limited, so Toshiko can quite rightly make a bad debt provision of £2,500 and will obtain tax relief for this in her June 2016 accounts.

VAT-registered businesses should only make provisions for the net, VAT-exclusive, part of the debt, as the VAT element is not part of your sales and can always be recovered or, in many cases, never paid.

Specific versus General

Some businesses make a 'general provision' to reflect the fact that there is always some doubt over the recovery of debts (e.g. 1% of all outstanding debts).

This is usually a bad idea, as a general provision is ineligible for tax relief, whereas a properly calculated specific provision does provide relief.

Example
Toshiko's other debtors at 30th June 2016 total £100,000. After her bad experience with Victim Limited, she decides to make a further provision of 2% against these other debts – i.e. £2,000.

In October, Toshiko passes her draft accounts to her accountant, Martha, who explains that, whilst Toshiko will get tax relief for the provision against Victim Limited's debt, she can't claim relief for her £2,000 general provision.

What Martha also does, however, is to review which of Toshiko's other debts at 30th June are also still outstanding. These sums are now more than 60 days overdue and total £8,000. Martha asks Toshiko if these amounts are likely to be recovered. "Possibly", replies Toshiko, "but I'd say there's about a one in four chance that they won't."

Martha therefore lists the outstanding debts, calculates a provision equal to 25% of the sums outstanding and includes this in Toshiko's accounts at 30th June instead of the 2% general provision.

Whilst Martha's provision is the same amount as Toshiko's general provision, it has been properly calculated on a specific basis and is therefore an allowable deduction for tax purposes.

A little extra effort in accounts preparation pays off in tax relief!

Timing of Relief

Where a debt, or any part of it, has almost certainly become irrecoverable, accounting principles require it to be written off or a specific provision to be made in the accounts. In some cases, however, where the recovery is merely doubtful, there may be some flexibility over the timing of tax relief.

Example
Toshiko's profits for the year ended 30th June 2016 were £40,000 before she made any bad debt provisions, but she anticipates a profit of £110,000 in the year ending 30th June 2017. This gives her an effective marginal rate of combined Income Tax and National Insurance of just 29% on her 2016 profit but a colossal 62% for 2017.

Making bad debt provisions in her 2016 accounts therefore saves tax at just 29%. Toshiko would be better off if she just waits to see whether she recovers these debts – any that do go bad during the year to 30th June 2017 will then provide tax relief at 62%.

Does It Really Matter?

Some people take the view that a bad debt is really just the same as a sale which never took place. This is not the case: there are several important differences.

Accounting principles require the sale to be recognised and total turnover, including these sales, is an important measure for many purposes, including the VAT registration threshold and Companies House filing requirements.

And, as we have seen, bad debts may sometimes yield tax relief at a higher rate than the tax on the original sale!

Bad Debts: VAT Relief

Many businesses with turnover of less than £1.6m operate the cash accounting scheme and don't account for VAT on their sales until they get paid. Relief for bad debts is therefore automatic.

For those not in the cash accounting scheme, a debt is 'bad' for VAT purposes when it is six months overdue. This means that the debt must be unpaid six months after the normal due date. Hence, if you normally give your customers a month to pay, the debt won't be 'bad' until seven months after an invoice is issued.

At this point, relief can be claimed for the VAT included in the bad debt by adding it to the total in 'Box 4' on the VAT Return as if it were VAT on a purchase.

If some or all of the debt is later recovered, the VAT element of the amount received must then be included in the business's output VAT in 'Box 1' of the VAT Return for the relevant period. The same rate of VAT as was charged on the original sale must be used to calculate the VAT element of any sums recovered.

If you're not in the cash accounting scheme, VAT creates an additional cashflow disadvantage on any bad debts. This may give you cause to hold off invoicing a customer if there appears to be little or no hope of getting paid. If you're on cash accounting though, there is nothing to lose.

Chapter 40

Accountants Make Mistakes

One of our readers contacted us a while ago with a shocking story. His accountant, when putting together his business tax return, disallowed £15,000 worth of perfectly legitimate business expenses without consultation.

Fortunately, the reader carefully checked a draft set of accounts before they were submitted and spotted the errors.

Most were very standard expenses but were disallowed simply because the accountant's assistant could not find the payments in the company's bank account and assumed they were not genuine expenses.

The two most important lessons from this story are:

- Nobody cares about your tax bill as much as you do.

- No matter how much careful tax planning you do, it's worthless if your accountant doesn't do their job correctly.

Fortunately, most accountants do not make mistakes on this scale and take pride in doing the best possible job. The problem experienced by our reader can be avoided by taking these steps:

- When you submit your annual income and expenses to your accountant, ask them to discuss any issues with you before disallowing any expenses (to save on fees, you may wish to set a minimum level for this – e.g. expenses over £100).

- When they send you a draft tax return, ask again whether any expenses have been disallowed.

- When you receive a draft tax return, check that the figures tally with the information you provided. This is relatively easy to do because most sole trader/partnership tax returns should contain a breakdown of your business costs.

- Provide additional information relating to expenses that are more likely to be disallowed. For example, if you spend money on repairs to your premises, you may want to explain more about the exact nature of the work undertaken so that your accountant can make a fully informed decision and discuss it with you.

- Hand over your accounts information early. If your accountant has to rush to meet the deadline, there is a greater chance that mistakes will be made or that there will be no time to consult with you.

- Do not use your accountant as your bookkeeper. It is usually not cost effective to pay your accountant to type up expenses, etc. You will save on fees, and possibly tax too, if you provide your accounting information in an organised format, such as on spreadsheets. Best of all, ask your accountant what information they would like, and in what format – working together produces the best results!

- Question your accountant about who will be doing the work.

- Ultimately, if you cannot get a satisfactory service, consider taking your business elsewhere.

If your business has significantly fewer transactions this year than last year, don't be shy to ask for a reduction in fees.

Finally, if checking over your tax return and accounts fills you with dread, remember that the flipside of this tale is equally worrying: If your accountant underestimates your tax bill, it is you who will be accountable. In the end, the final responsibility lies with you!

Part 12

VAT

Chapter 41

VAT Basics

Businesses are usually compulsorily required to register for VAT when their 'taxable' turnover in any 12 month period exceeds the VAT registration threshold.

Most forms of business sales will represent 'taxable' turnover for VAT purposes, although there are some exceptions.

The VAT registration threshold currently stands at £83,000.

Registering for VAT means that you will have to start adding VAT to your invoices – usually at the 'standard rate', which is currently 20% (although rates of 5% and 0% also sometimes apply). The good news, however, is that you can then also recover the VAT paid on many of your business expenses.

Voluntary Registration

It is also possible to voluntarily register for VAT. This may be desirable if your customers are VAT registered businesses themselves and don't mind VAT being added to the invoices you send them because they can simply reclaim the tax.

Registering for VAT will then allow you to reclaim the tax paid on your own business expenses.

For businesses that sell to private individuals, voluntary registration is often a bad idea because your customers cannot reclaim the VAT you charge them. You can either raise your prices and potentially lose customers or keep your prices fixed and earn less profit (because some of your revenue will be paid to HMRC).

The position is different for businesses making 'zero-rated' supplies, such as new housing, printed matter (books, magazines, etc.), or fresh food. The VAT rate applying is 0%, meaning that you can recover the VAT on your own purchases without increasing the charges to your customers. For these businesses, voluntary registration is generally a good idea.

VAT and Your Tax Deductible Expenses

If your business is not VAT registered, you can claim Income Tax and National Insurance relief on your total business expenses, including the VAT which you haven't been able to recover.

If your business is VAT registered, you can claim Income Tax and National Insurance relief on your net business expenses, after subtracting the VAT that has been reclaimed.

Example 1
Guy is a VAT registered sole trader and pays £100 + £20 VAT for some advice from a VAT registered accountant. He can reclaim the £20 VAT and claim the remaining £100 as a business tax deduction.

Example 2
James is a sole trader but not VAT registered. He also pays £100 + £20 VAT for some professional advice from a VAT registered accountant. He cannot reclaim the £20 VAT but can claim the entire £120 as a business tax deduction.

Calculating VAT Quickly

If you are quoted any price inclusive of 20% VAT and want to calculate the VAT component quickly, simply divide by six.

Example
Simon is quoted a price of £100, which includes 20% VAT. The VAT component is £16.67 (£100/6).

VAT Planning

We've showed you how to increase your VAT relief in various chapters of this guide including:

- Chapter 24 – claiming VAT back on certain motoring costs
- Chapter 25 – claiming VAT on fuel
- Chapter 27 – claiming VAT relief on lease payments

In the next two chapters we will look at some of the special VAT schemes available to small business owners.

Chapter 42

The VAT Flat Rate Scheme: Benefits & Drawbacks

Many businesses could benefit by taking a look at the flat rate scheme. For some, the scheme can save time and money; but watch out, for some, it can cost money!

The scheme allows you to account for VAT at a single flat rate on all your sales. This flat rate is reduced from the normal standard rate (currently 20%) to allow for the fact that you generally cannot claim the VAT on your purchases.

Not being able to recover VAT on your expenses is the price you pay for joining the scheme. You can claim the VAT on any capital purchases (furniture, machinery, equipment, etc) over £2,000 however.

The scheme is available to most businesses with annual sales (before VAT) of less than £150,000. You can leave the scheme at the end of any VAT quarter but cannot re-join within a year of leaving.

The flat rate you use is based on the type of business you have and can be found by following the link from:

www.gov.uk/vat-flat-rate-scheme

If you are in your first year of VAT registration you get a special discount – a one per cent reduction in your flat rate percentage. So the scheme is often beneficial when you first register as long as your purchases are not unusually high at this time.

The rates applying are not as generous as they look, however, as they are applied to your total, VAT-inclusive, sales prices.

Example
Dave sells a table for £100 plus VAT – a total of £120. He operates the flat rate scheme with a rate of 7.5% applying. He must therefore account for VAT of £9 (£120 x 7.5%).

Rates are set on an industry-wide basis and hence, in very general terms, it follows that you will benefit from the scheme if the VAT you pay on your purchases is less than your industry average.

This could arise for a number of reasons but the main things to watch out for are:

- Rent – if you don't pay rent for your business premises or don't pay VAT on it

- Labour – if you employ more people than average rather than paying VAT on sub-contractors' charges

- Goods – if you purchase more zero-rated or VAT-exempt items than is usual in your industry

The scheme has a few pitfalls to watch out for. You still have to account for VAT on imports of goods or services under the 'reverse charge' procedure and you cannot use the scheme if you have any associated businesses.

Worst of all, the 'VAT-registered entity' must account for VAT at the same rate on almost all business income of any kind. This would include rental income, for example, although bank interest may now be excluded.

This is a particular hazard for sole traders, since the individual is the VAT-registered entity.

Chapter 43

The Correct Retail Scheme Could Save You Thousands

Most retailers work largely with cash sales and do not generally produce invoices, so there is a need for a special system to calculate the amount of VAT due. Thus we have a number of 'retail schemes'.

Some retailers are large, some are small; some have more than one rate of VAT to account for, depending on their product list or the 'lines' they offer. Some retailers have complex computer systems and some operate very simply.

HM Revenue & Customs (HMRC) has therefore developed, over the years, a selection of schemes designed to suit most retailers. Large retailers are able to devise their own variations with the necessary approval of HMRC.

Smaller retailers must choose one of five basic schemes. There may be more than one scheme available and, just because one scheme works well for one particular shop, another retailer might be much better off choosing a different scheme.

The schemes are subject to a number of conditions and some are not suitable for some types of business. Others are subject to turnover thresholds. You will therefore need to check the conditions which apply before choosing an appropriate scheme.

Note that the retail schemes are only used to determine the VAT due on sales. The deductible VAT incurred on purchases is calculated in the normal way and is unaffected by the choice of scheme.

As a further alternative, however, small retailers with annual turnover of no more than £150,000 (excluding VAT) may use the flat rate scheme (see Chapter 42).

The only retail scheme that, in theory, produces a truly accurate VAT result is the 'point of sale' scheme, which basically records every sale with a proper VAT code. This is normally carried out via an electronic till and is then referred to as the EPOS (electronic point of sale) method.

Where such facilities are not available, the other schemes offer calculation methods as follows:

Apportionment Schemes

Scheme 1: Under this method, you simply split the gross takings for the period in the same ratio as your VAT-inclusive purchases under the different liability rates (standard, reduced, or zero). The VAT included in your sales can then be worked out as appropriate.

This sounds fairly reasonable but the important point to note is that if, on average, you have a higher profit margin on zero-rated goods than on standard-rated goods, then you will end up paying more VAT using this scheme because it does not take profit margins into consideration. This aspect of the scheme is often overlooked.

Scheme 2: This scheme is based on the 'expected sales price' (ESP) of goods purchased and again applies the ratio, established from the total purchases under each category, to the retailer's gross takings.

Thus, for example, if the ratio of total ESPs for goods purchased was 50/50 between standard-rated and zero-rated goods, then you would take 50% of your gross sales as being standard-rated and the VAT due would be one sixth of that value (based on the current standard rate of VAT: 20%).

This scheme effectively does take your profit margins into account and will therefore produce a better result than Scheme 1 above where the margin on your zero-rated sales is generally higher than on standard-rated sales.

Direct Calculation Schemes

Scheme 1: First, you establish the total ESP of goods purchased subject to the VAT rate which applies to the fewest sales. You then subtract this total from your gross takings to leave the VAT-inclusive total for your remaining sales. For example:

Gross takings in VAT period	£30,000
Zero-rated purchases marked up to sales value	£12,000
Balance of sales deemed to be standard-rated	£18,000
VAT due: £18,000/6	£3,000

If you have sales at all three VAT rates, you will need to calculate totals for the two rates producing the fewer sales and deduct both of these from your gross takings to provide a VAT-inclusive total for the sales made at your most common VAT rate.

Scheme 2: This operates in much the same way as Scheme 1 above, but is subject to an annual stock adjustment.

Choosing a Scheme

Having checked the relevant conditions for each scheme, you may find that you have more than one choice. Before selecting a scheme, it may be wise to take a look at how it would work out based on the purchases and sales made in a typical VAT period.

For example, let's suppose you have gross takings of £135,000, standard-rated purchases of £50,000 (including VAT) and zero-rated purchases of £50,000. The mark-up on your standard-rated goods is 20% and the mark-up on your zero-rated goods is 50%.

Using Apportionment Scheme 1, you would split your gross takings 50/50, giving you VAT-inclusive standard-rated sales of £67,500. The VAT due would thus be £67,500/6 = £11,250.

If, however, Direct Calculation Scheme 1 was used instead, you would calculate your total standard-rated sales as £50,000 + 20% = £60,000. The VAT due would then be £60,000/6 = £10,000.

Simply choosing the right scheme could therefore save you over £1,000 – every quarter!

Part 13

Capital Gains Tax

Chapter 44

Entrepreneurs' Relief

One of the most tax-efficient ways to grow your wealth is to build and then sell several businesses during your working life.

This allows you to convert streams of heavily taxed income into low-taxed capital gains.

At present, business owners who earn over £100,000 face marginal personal tax rates of up to 62% on their income. The many higher-rate taxpayers out there (those earning over £43,000 in 2016/17) face a marginal tax rate of at least 42%.

But, when you sell a business and receive a big cash lump sum, which replaces all this heavily taxed income, you could end up paying less than 10% tax if you qualify for Capital Gains Tax Entrepreneurs' Relief.

Although serial entrepreneurs pay much less tax than other business owners, that lifestyle is not for everyone. Nevertheless, every business owner will benefit from a basic understanding of the special Capital Gains Tax rules that apply to people in business, especially Entrepreneurs' Relief.

Why? Because if you do eventually cash in your chips, there are certain things you need to check and do before you sell.

Entrepreneurs' Relief can save a couple up to £2 million in Capital Gains Tax, so it's worth knowing what you have to do to protect it.

How Entrepreneurs' Relief Works

Up to £10 million of capital gains per person can qualify for Entrepreneurs' Relief.

This is a lifetime limit but can be used for more than one business sale.

Because Entrepreneurs' Relief applies on a per person basis, the more people who own the business (your spouse or partner, children, etc), the more tax you could save!

Sole traders, partnerships and company owners may all potentially qualify but, in each case, the business has to be what the taxman refers to as a "trade". Generally speaking this means that investment businesses (e.g. property investment businesses) do not qualify.

Furthermore, to qualify, the business must have been owned for at least one year.

Sole traders are generally only entitled to Entrepreneurs' Relief when they sell the whole business (or shut it down and sell off the assets). If you continue trading but sell some business assets, for example a piece of intellectual property or your trading premises, you will not be entitled to any Entrepreneurs' Relief.

The only way a sole trader can sell part of a business and still potentially qualify for Entrepreneurs' Relief is if that part is capable of operating as a going concern in its own right (for example, an office or shop in another town). However, HMRC is taking a very strict line on this issue, so it is not something to be relied upon without taking professional advice.

Selling Property

Many business owners purchase business premises personally and rent them back to their company or partnership (this does not apply to sole traders because they cannot rent their own properties).

The good news is that Entrepreneurs' Relief is available when "associated" assets like these are sold as part of an overall sale of the business. The bad news is that many business owners will not qualify for the maximum tax relief.

If the company or partnership pays you rent in respect of any period after 5th April 2008, your Entrepreneurs' Relief will be restricted. The taxman's reasoning is that if the property is only available if rent is paid, it is an investment asset and not a business asset.

There are two pieces of good news here though. Firstly, any rent receivable before April 2008 is disregarded and, secondly, rent paid at less than the market rate only leads to a partial reduction in the available Entrepreneurs' Relief.

For example, the gain on a property owned since 5th April 2005 and rented to the owner's partnership business for 50% of market rent until its sale (as part of a larger business sale) 12 years later, on 5th April 2017, would have its Entrepreneurs' Relief restricted by a factor of 9/12 x 50% = 37.5%. (E.g. if the gain were £100,000, relief could be claimed on £62,500 of that gain.)

Tax Planning Pointers

Beware of Incorporating

If you have a sole trader business or partnership, you should be wary of incorporating (putting the business into a company) within one year of selling. To qualify for Entrepreneurs' Relief, you have to own the shares of the newly formed company for at least one year.

Be Wary of Business Transfers to Family Members

Transfers to spouses are exempt from CGT and can save significant amounts of Income Tax. However, if the business is sold less than one year after the transfer, Entrepreneurs' Relief will not be available on the transferred share unless the spouse already held a share of the business before that (and for at least a year prior to the sale).

Chapter 45

How to Pay 10% Tax on Investment Property

Entrepreneurs' Relief lets you pay 10% tax on up to £10 million of capital gains during your lifetime.

With the top Capital Gains Tax rate now 20% for assets other than residential property, the potential saving is £1 million per person.

The relief is designed mainly for people selling businesses, in particular 'trading businesses'. A trading business is, for want of a better word, a 'regular' business, as opposed to an investment business which owns assets like rental properties.

Entrepreneurs' Relief is not generally available when you sell investment properties but it may be available when you sell properties used in a trading business, for example your premises.

Fortunately, you may be able to convert an investment property into a trading property in certain circumstances and benefit from the 10% tax rate.

Entrepreneurs' Relief is generally available if you are using the property in a trading business at the time that you sell or close down the business (known as a cessation) and you had carried on that business for at least a year before that time.

In cases of cessation, the property must be sold within three years of the cessation.

So the basic principle is this: set up a business for a year, use your property in the business, sell the business or close it down, claim Entrepreneurs' Relief on the property sale.

The Structure of the Business

This strategy will not work so well if the business you set up is a company or partnership.

When you sell a property that was used by your company or partnership, this is known as an associated disposal. The Entrepreneurs' Relief available on an associated disposal is restricted to reflect any period when the asset was not being used in a qualifying business carried on by the company or partnership.

In other words, if you've owned the property for 20 years and your company uses it for one year, at best you will receive Entrepreneurs' Relief on just 5% of your gain.

However, no such restrictions apply where the property is used by a sole trader in their own trading business or as qualifying furnished holiday accommodation. In these cases, it appears that full Entrepreneurs' Relief is available: provided that the property is being used in the business when the business is sold or there is a cessation.

Where the owner has an existing qualifying business, it even appears that there is no minimum period for which the property must be used in that business, provided that the owner runs the business itself for at least a year.

For those without an existing qualifying business, it will be necessary to set one up and run it for at least a year in order to benefit.

Example
In 1982, Abdul bought a shop as an investment property for £30,000. It is now worth £330,000 and he would like to sell it.

Before selling the property, however, Abdul adopts it as his own trading premises for thirteen months. He then ceases trading and sells the property, making a gain of £300,000.

Because Abdul used the property in his own trade, he will be entitled to Entrepreneurs' Relief, reducing the Capital Gains Tax due on his sale from £60,000 to £30,000 (ignoring the annual CGT exemption and assuming that Abdul is a higher-rate taxpayer).

The important point to note is that Abdul still gets the relief despite the fact that the entire gain arose before he adopted the property as his own trading premises!

Note that Abdul would need to use the property in his own qualifying trade – e.g. as a shop with him as sole proprietor. Using it as the office for his investment business will not suffice. He can, however, employ a manager to run the shop for him if he wishes.

To determine whether this tax saving strategy will be worthwhile, you will need to weigh up the potential tax savings against the costs (lost rental income, business rates and any other costs associated with setting up, running and then shutting down the business).

In the right circumstances, however, you could save thousands in Capital Gains Tax.

Part 14

Inheritance Tax

Chapter 46

Business Property Relief: Avoiding the Grave Robbers

There is a very important relief called 'business property relief', which often shelters the value of business assets from the scourge of Inheritance Tax.

This relief is one of the most important tax reliefs for business owners in the UK which is why, in the next two chapters, we are looking at how to benefit from it, how to maximise the savings arising and, perhaps most importantly of all, how to make sure that you do not accidentally lose it!

Digging Deep

Let's start by looking at the size of the problem. When most UK taxpayers die, subject to certain exemptions (including business property relief), the entire value of their estate in excess of the 'nil rate band' is taxed at 40%.

In other words, even though you will have paid tax all your life, the Government will still want to deprive your rightful heirs of up to 40% of their inheritance!

Whatever their background, there is much that all politicians have in common. Labour reneged on a commitment to increase the nil rate band and put in place a five year freeze; the Conservatives then dropped their pledge to increase it to £1m, adopted Labour's freeze instead, and then extended the freeze for a further three years.

The end result is that the nil rate band is set to remain at just £325,000 until at least 5th April 2018. Allowing for inflation, its real value by that time will be considerably less, thus exposing a great many more people to Inheritance Tax and adding to the burden falling on those who are caught.

'Coffin Up'

Perhaps the best way to illustrate the importance of business property relief is to look at what would happen without it.

Example
Leslie owns a house currently worth £275,000 and a share in a small business manufacturing parts for vintage aeroplanes, also currently worth £275,000. We will assume that Leslie's business share will not qualify for business property relief on his death.

Leslie's current Inheritance Tax exposure amounts to £90,000. This is derived by deducting the nil rate band of £325,000 from the total value of Leslie's estate, £550,000, and multiplying the resultant figure (£225,000) by 40%.

Let us now suppose that Leslie's assets increase in line with inflation and, by April 2018, his house and business share are each worth £300,000.

Leslie dies on 5th April 2018. If he had been entitled to business property relief on his business share, its value would have been exempt from Inheritance Tax. His house alone would have been covered by the nil rate band, leaving his executors with no Inheritance Tax to pay.

As things stand, however, Leslie's entire estate, worth £600,000, is exposed to Inheritance Tax. After deducting the nil rate band (still just £325,000), he is left with £275,000 to be taxed at 40%, yielding an Inheritance Tax bill of £110,000.

As we can see from the example, without business property relief, even a fairly small business would give rise to a significant Inheritance Tax bill. Poor Leslie is worth just £550,000 today but pure inflation alone could give his executors a tax bill of well over £100,000 by 2018.

Till Death Do Us Part

At this stage I should point out that things may not be quite so bad if you are married. Assets you leave to your spouse or civil partner are generally exempt from Inheritance Tax.

Furthermore, if you don't use your nil rate band, you will effectively leave that to them too (any part of the nil rate band which is not used on a married person's death transfers to their spouse or civil partner).

Even so, without business property relief this generally only delays the problem. A couple with more than £650,000 of assets would still be exposed to Inheritance Tax on the second spouse's death.

For those who are single or divorced, their Inheritance Tax exposure, like Leslie's, starts at a much lower level. Anyone married to a foreign national may face increased exposure too: the exemption for transfers to your spouse will sometimes then be limited to just £325,000 (no coincidence: this exemption is set at the same level as the nil rate band).

On top of this there is the fact that you may prefer to pass your business directly to your children, or other heirs, rather than your spouse.

In short, whilst the spouse exemption is extremely useful, in the end it is no substitute for business property relief!

What Assets Qualify for Business Property Relief?

In effect, there are three requirements which you need to meet in order to qualify for business property relief:

- You need to have a qualifying business

- You need to hold relevant business property

- You need to meet the minimum holding period requirement

A qualifying business for this purpose generally means a business which is wholly or mainly a 'trading business'. Most regular businesses that sell goods or services are trading businesses, as opposed to, for example, businesses that derive most of their income from holding investments.

Professions, such as lawyers, accountants, doctors, dentists, etc, also generally qualify for business property relief.

The minimum holding period is generally two years. So if you have owned a trading business, or a share in it, for more than two years, this will generally qualify.

The term 'relevant business property' refers to the way in which you own the business, or your share in it. The amount of business property relief which you are entitled to is dependent on the type of relevant business property you have.

Several of the most common business structures yield 100% relief:

    i)   A sole trader business
    ii)   A share in a partnership (including an LLP)
    iii)   Unquoted company shares
    iv)   Unquoted securities (e.g. loan stock) in a company which, either alone, or together with other unquoted shares or securities, give you control of that company

In the following cases, however, the relief is restricted to just 50%:

    v)   Quoted shares or securities in a company which, either alone or together with other quoted shares or securities, give you control of that company
    vi)   Assets which you hold personally (or held on your behalf by certain types of trust), which are used by a company under your control, or a partnership in which you are a partner

In broad terms, therefore, most sole traders, business partners and owners of unquoted companies will be entitled to 100% business property relief. Remember, however, that, whatever business structure is used, there must also be a qualifying business.

In the Pit

There are numerous pitfalls which can lead to the loss of business property relief and expose your family to an Inheritance Tax bill equal to up to 40% of the value of your business.

For example, in a partnership, a partner's capital account may qualify for business property relief but a loan account (e.g. if money has been lent to the partnership) generally will not. This is a particular problem with many Limited Liability Partnerships.

252

It is also worth noting that partners who hold business assets personally outside the partnership only get 50% relief on those assets.

This situation most often arises in the case of business premises which, for other reasons, are sometimes held personally. Those 'other reasons' are often very good ones but the impact on the business owner's business property relief should be taken into account.

Borrowings: Another Pitfall

Business liabilities, such as business overdrafts and trade creditors, have always reduced the value of a business eligible for business property relief.

Until recently, however, this did not extend to personal liabilities incurred by a business owner to finance their business: such as personal loans or a mortgage over their own home.

Sadly, new rules introduced in 2013 mean that *any* liabilities incurred to finance the acquisition, enhancement or maintenance of a qualifying business, must now be taken to reduce the value of that business (subject to the comments below regarding liabilities incurred before 6th April 2013).

A liability will be deemed to have financed a business where it is used directly or indirectly for that purpose. Guidance issued by HMRC indicates that they are taking a very broad view of what can be taken to have been used to indirectly finance a business.

Liabilities Incurred Before 6th April 2013

Non-business liabilities incurred before 6th April 2013 are exempt from the new rules and may generally continue to be deducted in full from the general assets of the deceased business owner's estate.

However, where a liability incurred before 6th April 2013 is refinanced or varied on or after that date it will be treated as a new liability and it will then be caught by the new rules.

Replacing or varying any mortgages, personal loans, or other non-business liabilities incurred before 6th April 2013 which have been used, directly or indirectly, to finance your business could therefore lead to significant increases in your Inheritance Tax liability.

Coming in to Land

To close this chapter, let's go back to our main example to see how business property relief is calculated.

Example Revisited

Let us now suppose that Leslie managed to change things before he died, so that his business did qualify for business property relief. Let us also suppose, however, that his business share was made up of a partnership share worth £100,000 and the partnership's trading premises, worth £200,000, which Leslie owned personally. His Inheritance Tax calculation will now be as follows:

Chargeable assets:	
House	£300,000
Partnership share	£100,000
Business property relief (100%)	(£100,000)
Trading premises	£200,000
Business property relief (50%)	(£100,000)
Total:	£400,000

Deducting the nil rate band (£325,000) leaves £75,000 chargeable at 40%, giving Leslie's estate an Inheritance Tax bill of £30,000.

Chapter 47

How to Safeguard Your Business Property Relief

Do you want to give the Government 40% of your business?

No? Well, in that case, you need to make sure you don't make one of the common errors that could lead to the loss of your business property relief (BPR).

In the previous chapter we saw that, without BPR, your heirs could effectively lose 40% of your entire estate in excess of a nil rate band of just £325,000 on your death. Where your business does qualify for BPR, however, its entire value will often be exempt from Inheritance Tax.

Losing Out

The difference it can make to your heirs if your business qualifies for BPR is enormous. Let's say you have other assets worth over £325,000 (highly likely, as your house is included) and a business worth £10m. Without BPR, your estate will have to pay an Inheritance Tax bill of over £4m: enough to cripple your business. With the relief, you can effectively pass the business on tax free.

So, it's vital to keep the relief available whenever possible. Generally speaking, this means that you will need to have owned qualifying business assets for at least two years.

Under the 'replacement property' provisions, however, you would retain full BPR as long as you owned qualifying business assets for a total period of at least two years during the five year period prior to your death. In effect, this gives you up to three years to reinvest the sale proceeds of a qualifying business into a new qualifying business without any loss of BPR. Provided that you actually do own qualifying business assets at the time of your death, that is!

The problem, of course, is that it is generally pretty unpredictable when this will be. Furthermore, it may be some time after you cease to be interested in running a business. Most people will want to retire at some point and, unfortunately, this will often result in the loss of the relief.

Selling Up

As soon as you have a binding contract for sale, you are, for Inheritance Tax purposes, no longer regarded as owning the asset being sold. Instead, you are regarded as owning a right to the sale proceeds.

That right is generally not a qualifying asset for BPR purposes. Hence, at one stroke of a pen, you can lose your BPR and substantially increase your family's Inheritance Tax bill in the event of your death.

Example
Eddie owns a trading business. The business is Eddie's only asset so, as things stand, he has no need to worry about Inheritance Tax.

Eddie gets an offer from a French company to buy his business for £10,325,000. He decides to accept the offer, so he flies to Paris, takes the Metro to the French company's offices and signs a binding contract to sell his business.

Leaving the office, Eddie looks the wrong way crossing the street and steps in front of a bus. Inheritance Tax bill: £4m!

This is based on a true story and readily demonstrates the ease with which BPR can be lost and the dire consequences that may result.

An entrepreneur like Eddie might well have been intending to reinvest his sale proceeds in a new business venture and hence might have regained the protection of BPR within a few weeks by virtue of the 'replacement property' provisions.

Perhaps Eddie should have considered taking out some insurance to cover the Inheritance Tax risk during this short interval!

Retirement

BPR is lost as soon as a partner retires from a qualifying partnership business. Any capital that the retired partner leaves in the business is simply regarded as a loan.

One way to avoid this problem is for the partner to continue in partnership, but with a very small profit share. (Remaining in partnership has commercial implications, which should also be considered.)

When a sole trader retires there is no business so there can be no BPR. The answer here may be to take on a partner and then, at a later date, to 'semi-retire' – i.e. reduce to a very small profit share in the manner described above.

An individual owning qualifying shares in an unquoted trading company can happily retire without any loss of BPR, as their position depends on their shareholding and not on whether they actually participate in the company's business. Incorporating the business prior to retirement may therefore sometimes be another good way to preserve BPR.

Buy-Out Clauses: A BIG NO-NO!

It is common business practice for business partners to enter into an agreement whereby their executors will sell their partnership share to the surviving partners in the event of their death.

Similar agreements are also often used by shareholder/directors of unquoted companies whereby their executors sell their shares back to the company, or to their fellow directors, in the event of their death.

Whilst these agreements make a good deal of commercial sense, from a BPR perspective, they represent a disaster waiting to happen. This is because, at the moment of death, a binding sale contract will come into force and the estate will not hold qualifying business property but, as we saw for Eddie above, will instead hold a non-qualifying right to sale proceeds.

It is therefore essential to avoid any form of agreement that may form a binding contract on the death of a partner or director.

Cross Options

A far better alternative is to use non-coterminous cross options.

In other words, the business partners should enter into an agreement whereby, in the event of a partner's death, their executors will have an option to sell the deceased's partnership share and the surviving partners will have an option to buy it.

Similarly, private company directors would enter into an agreement whereby, in the event of a director's death, their executors will have an option to sell the deceased's shares in the company and either the company itself or the surviving directors will have an option to buy them.

To be on the safe side, it is wise to ensure that the options are 'non-coterminous'. Broadly, this means that the option to purchase and the option to sell may only be exercised at different times. (E.g. the deceased's executors must exercise the option to sell within six weeks of the deceased's death and the surviving business partners, or directors, must exercise the option to purchase more than six, but less than twelve, weeks after the deceased's death.)

HM Revenue and Customs has confirmed that this approach is acceptable in the case of a business partnership and there is no reason to suppose that the same principles would not be equally valid in the case of company shares.

Using cross options will therefore preserve full BPR entitlement whilst also satisfying the commercial objective of allowing the deceased's share of a business to be 'bought out'.

Part 15

Other Important Tax Issues

Chapter 48

Benefits and Drawbacks of Cash Accounting

Individuals and partnerships with small trading businesses can elect to be taxed under the 'cash basis' (also known as 'cash accounting'). This 'cash accounting' is not to be confused with the VAT scheme discussed in Chapter 39, which is also called 'cash accounting'!

The 'cash basis' is generally only available where the annual turnover (i.e. sales) of the business does not exceed the VAT registration threshold (currently £83,000); although those who are already using the 'cash basis' may continue to do so provided their turnover does not exceed twice the VAT registration threshold (i.e. £166,000 at current rates).

Businesses electing to use the 'cash basis' are taxed simply on the difference between business income received during the year and business expenses paid during the year, instead of under normal accounting principles.

Where the 'cash basis' is used, there is no distinction between 'revenue expenditure' and 'capital expenditure' and capital expenditure may simply be claimed as it is paid, except that:

- Expenditure on the purchase of cars is not allowed on a cash basis. Motor expenses must continue to be claimed under one of the two alternative methods described in Chapter 22.

- The cost of vans or motor cycles may be claimed on a cash basis but if the purchase cost is claimed this way, the mileage allowances (see Chapter 26) will not be available.

- Capital expenditure may only be claimed under the 'cash basis' where it would otherwise normally qualify for capital allowances as 'plant and machinery' (see Chapter 16).

In addition to these restrictions, businesses using the 'cash basis' are limited to a maximum claim of £500 per year in respect of interest on cash borrowings.

Losses arising under the 'cash basis' can only be carried forward for set off against future profits from the same trade and are not eligible for any other form of loss relief.

In view of these restrictions, and the turnover limits described above, it seems unlikely that the 'cash basis' will benefit many small businesses.

The Thin End of the Wedge?

The Government claims that the 'cash basis' makes accounting simpler for small businesses and reduces a great deal of the administrative burden on them.

Personally, I have my doubts and, although the scheme is meant to be voluntary, there are signs that it could represent the 'thin end of the wedge' and may herald a move towards a more aggressive approach to the taxation of small businesses, with far less recognition of the unique and special nature of each business and its owner in the future.

The Government is promoting the new accounting method on the basis of its 'simplicity' but, in my view, it still leaves most small businesses facing most of the same complexities that they faced before. Using it could also leave many small business owners worse off.

Restricting interest relief for business borrowings will act as a major disincentive to any small business seeking to grow. How does that fit in with the Government's enterprise agenda?

A Simple Idea?

The basic idea is simple enough. Under the cash accounting method income is taxable when it is received and expenditure is deductible when it is paid. So, in effect, the theory is that there is no need to worry about debtors, creditors, accruals, prepayments, or stock valuations.

The additional benefit (in theory) is that expenditure on equipment, machinery, and most other items will be allowed when it is paid, with no need to distinguish between 'revenue' and 'capital' expenditure.

All these things are just a matter of timing, so the idea is that the business will be no better or worse off in the end, even though the amount of profit which is taxed in any given year may change.

But timing is SO important! Most business owners are much more concerned about how much tax they will have to pay this year than whether they are going to pay the same amount of tax between now and when they sell up!

The First Red Herring

Cash accounting is available to sole traders and partnerships with annual sales not exceeding the VAT registration threshold (currently £83,000). It is not available to companies, Limited Liability Partnerships, other partnerships which are not composed entirely of individuals, or property businesses (i.e. landlords).

So, the first 'red herring' to highlight is the so-called 'benefit' of not needing to distinguish between 'revenue' and 'capital' expenditure. Most businesses can currently claim an immediate 100% deduction on at least £200,000 of qualifying capital expenditure. This should be more than enough to cover most expenditure by any business with annual sales of £83,000 or less.

Hence, as far as capital expenditure is concerned, very few small businesses would see any difference if they used cash accounting.

For Better or Worse?

To assess whether cash accounting might be beneficial for your business, the first step is to consider what the impact on the timing of your business profits is likely to be. In other words, will profits generally be accelerated and taxed earlier, or will they generally be deferred and taxed later?

Under cash accounting, you will not be taxed on your debtors (sales you have made but not been paid for yet). You will also be able to claim a full deduction for expenses that you have paid, without any adjustments for closing stock or prepayments.

However, you will not be able to claim a deduction for business creditors (purchases made but not paid yet) or accruals (expenses that relate to the period of trading but which will arise later).

Example

Rose opens a new shop on 6th April 2016. In the year to 5th April 2017, she takes £60,000 in sales and makes the following expense payments:

Rent	*£13,000*
Electricity	*£2,000*
Equipment	*£4,000*
Insurance	*£2,000*
Stock purchases	*£20,000*

If Rose uses the cash accounting method, she will have a 'profit' for tax purposes of £19,000.

Under normal accounting methods, however, Rose would have a few adjustments to make. Firstly, she would not claim her equipment purchases as an expense but would instead claim capital allowances of the same amount – hence the 'red herring' referred to above, as there is no overall effect on her taxable profits.

Next, Rose would need to reduce her expense claims to take account of:

Prepaid rent for 6th to 30th April 2017 - £833
Prepaid insurance relating to period post-5th April 2017 - £500
Stock on hand at 5th April 2017 - £4,000

However, she would also increase her expense claims for:

Unpaid electricity bill - £500
Trade creditors (goods purchased not yet paid for) - £6,000
Accountancy fee accrual - £1,500

Finally, she would also reduce her sales to take account of goods returned after 5th April 2017, £333.

These adjustments would reduce her overall taxable profit to £16,000, saving her at least £870 in Income Tax and National Insurance.

As we can see, Rose would be worse off under the cash accounting method in her first year of trading since she would be taxed on a higher business profit.

I am not for a second suggesting that this would always be the case. It happened in Rose's case mainly because her:

- Business creditors and expense accruals

Were greater than her:

- Business debtors, closing stock value and expense prepayments

And this is the comparison which every business needs to make in order to initially determine whether cash accounting *might* be beneficial for them.

In short, it will generally come down to a question of whether debtors and stock (current assets) tend to be greater than creditors and accruals (current liabilities).

At this stage, it is worth pointing out that this is often where a good accountant proves their worth, by making the adjustments which correctly reflect all of the true costs of the trading period, thus reducing the value of current assets and making sure that all of the relevant liabilities are taken into account. This, in turn, brings the trading profits down to the correct level – but the scope to do this will be lost under the cash accounting method!

Nonetheless, even after all of these adjustments, there will be some businesses where the comparison made above will go the opposite way to Rose's and these businesses might benefit from cash accounting – but only 'might': because there are a few additional problems to be considered!

Cash Accounting Restrictions

Any business adopting the cash accounting method is limited to a maximum annual claim of £500 for interest on cash borrowings (business loans and overdrafts) and other associated costs such as loan arrangement fees. Other interest costs, such as hire purchase interest, mortgage interest on business premises, and credit card interest on purchases of business assets will generally be allowable.

Well that's simple isn't it? Buy a piece of equipment on HP and you get the interest allowed; take out a bank loan to buy it and you may be denied any relief for the interest. Really simple, yeah!

Example Part 2

Rose took out a five-year loan of £20,000 to get her business started. She paid a loan arrangement fee of £500. She also has a business overdraft facility of £5,000 for which she paid a fee of £90. During the year to 5th April 2017, she incurred £300 in interest on her overdraft and £1,200 on her loan.

Under normal accounting rules, Rose may claim the following deductions for these items:

Loan arrangement fee (1/5th)	*£100*
Overdraft fee	*£90*
Interest (£300 + £1,200)	*£1,500*
Total:	*£1,690*

These reduce her taxable profit for the year to 5th April 2017 to just £14,310 (£16,000 - £1,690).

Under the cash accounting method, she is restricted to a claim of just £500 to cover all of these items. This leaves her with a taxable profit of £18,500 (£19,000 - £500), £4,190 more than under normal accounting principles.

This would probably cost her at least £1,215 in additional Income Tax and National Insurance. Furthermore, the differences relating to interest and finance costs are not just a matter of timing: these are permanent restrictions in Rose's deductible expenditure.

On the plus side, it is worth noting that a deduction of up to £500 may still be claimed where the business owner incurs interest costs which are only partly for business purposes.

For example, if interest of £1,000 were incurred on a bank loan taken out to finance the purchase of equipment used only 25% for business purposes, normal principles would restrict the deductible expense to just £250, but a business using cash accounting could claim £500.

Nonetheless, the **total** deduction for all interest and finance costs on cash borrowings is still restricted to just £500 per year.

More Red Herrings

Let's dispel a few more 'simplification' myths, shall we?

Under cash accounting, a business proprietor will still need to keep a mileage log if they wish to claim any allowances for use of a car, van or motorcycle.

They will still need to record all business income and expenditure, albeit on a cash basis, and despite not having to worry about capital allowances calculations, they will still only be able to claim expenditure on items of equipment, machinery, furniture, etc, which would have qualified for capital allowances under normal principles. Private use adjustments will also still be required, where relevant.

In my experience, the hardest part of preparing accounts for most small business owners is not deciding **when** something can be claimed, but **whether** it can be claimed. It takes the average business owner moments to understand the idea of when income is earned and when expenses are incurred, but it has taken me most of my adult life to understand all the nuances of which expenses are allowable for tax purposes!

Cash accounting takes away only the trivial complexities of timing and leaves most of the other problems in place whilst also denying many perfectly legitimate deductions such as bank interest in excess of £500.

And, worst of all, when the business owner needs a set of accounts for anything else: a bank loan, student grant application for their children, potential business sale, or just to understand whether their business is really making a profit, they will still have to produce proper accounts anyway!

Cash Accounting Losses

'Negative' results (i.e. losses) arising under the cash accounting method will only be available to carry forward for relief against future profits from the same trade. This means that business owners cannot claim relief for trading losses against other income arising in the same year or the previous one. New business owners will also be denied the opportunity to carry losses back for relief against other income in the previous three years.

Chapter 49

Avoiding the Child Benefit Charge

As explained in Chapter 2, many parents are now suffering a draconian new tax charge, the High Income Child Benefit Charge, on income between £50,000 and £60,000. This creates the truly horrendous tax rates set out in the table in Chapter 2.

Many of the tax planning strategies outlined in this guide can be used to reduce a business owner's taxable income. When that business owner has income between £50,000 and £60,000 and is subject to the High Income Child Benefit Charge, the savings will be far greater than for most other taxpayers.

For example, a business owner with income of £60,000 and three children of school age, who simply carries out £10,000 worth of roof repairs at their business premises before their accounting date, would save £6,701!

If the same business owner's income is not in the £50,000 to £60,000 tax bracket in the following year, £2,501 of this saving would be a permanent saving.

Most of the people affected by the High Income Child Benefit Charge will be couples. This provides additional scope for savings: particularly focussing on some of the techniques which we looked at in Chapter 5 where a business owner is effectively able to divert some of their income to their spouse or partner.

Example

In the first example in Chapter 5, we saw how Colin and Bonnie were able to make tax savings when Colin involved Bonnie in his business.

Let us now suppose that Colin and Bonnie also have four children of school age.

Colin began with income of £60,000 before undertaking any planning. In the first part of our example, the couple saved a net sum of £1,935 when Colin paid Bonnie a salary of £15,922. Taking the High Income Child Benefit Charge into account would increase this saving to £5,149.

Later, we saw that the couple could save £2,789 if Colin gave Bonnie a partnership share. Taking the High Income Child Benefit Charge into account would increase this saving to £6,003.

Naturally, it also follows that any business owner who is suffering the High Income Child Benefit Charge must have some children: so the strategies for employing children discussed in Chapter 6 may also be useful in reducing the charge.

Example
Sarah's business makes a profit of £60,000. She has five children qualifying for child benefit so, as things stand, she will suffer a High Income Child Benefit Charge of £3,926.

Sarah's three eldest children help her out in her business from time to time. She decides to put this on a more formal footing and pays them salaries totalling £10,000.

The salary payments to her children enable Sarah to avoid the High Income Child Benefit Charge. Her total tax saving amounts to £8,126, meaning that the net cost of paying her children is a mere £1,874!

Chapter 50

The Tax Relief 'Cap'

From 2013/14 onwards, there is an annual limit on the total combined amount of Income Tax relief available under a number of different reliefs.

The limit applies where the loss, or other source of the relief, arises in 2013/14 or a later tax year (regardless of which year the relief is claimed for).

The total amount of relief which any individual may claim under all of these reliefs taken together in any one tax year is now limited to the greater of:

- £50,000, or
- 25% of their 'adjusted total income' (see below)

Hence, for anyone with total income of no more £200,000, the limit is £50,000.

The Affected Reliefs

Ten different reliefs are affected. The most important ones for business owners to be aware of are:

- Relief for trading losses against other income
- Qualifying loan interest
- Share loss relief
- Property loss relief

Individuals with trading losses can set them off against their other income in the same tax year or the previous one. Additional relief applies in the early years of a trade.

'Qualifying loan interest' is the relief which is given for interest on personal borrowings used to invest funds in a qualifying company or partnership. See Chapter 28 for further details.

'Share loss relief' applies in certain limited circumstances and allows owners of some private companies to claim Income Tax relief for losses on their shares.

'Property loss relief' refers to an individual's ability to set capital allowances within UK rental losses or overseas rental losses against their other income for the same tax year or the next one.

Adjusted Total Income

Broadly speaking, 'adjusted total income' means an individual's total taxable income for the tax year in which relief is being claimed; after deducting gross pension contributions (including tax relief given at source); but before deducting any other reliefs.

Appendix

UK Tax Rates and Allowances: 2015/16 to 2017/18

	Rates	2015/16 £	2016/17 £	2017/18 £
Income Tax				
Personal allowance		10,600	11,000	11,500
Basic rate band	20%	31,785	32,000	33,500(1)
Higher rate/Threshold	40%	42,385	43,000	45,000(1)
Personal allowance withdrawal				
Effective rate/From	60%	100,000	100,000	100,000
To		121,200	122,000	123,000
Additional rate/Threshold	45%	150,000	150,000	150,000
Starting rate band (2)	0%	5,000	5,000	5,000
Marriage allowance (3)		1,060	1,100	1,150
Personal savings allowance (4)		n/a	1,000	1,000
Dividend allowance		n/a	5,000	5,000
National Insurance				
Primary threshold	%/12%	8,060	8,060	Unknown
Upper earnings limit	2%	42,385	43,000	45,000
Secondary threshold	13.8%	8,112	8,112	Unknown
Employment allowance		2,000	3,000	3,000
Class 2 – per week		2.80	2.80	Unknown
Small profits threshold		5,965	5,965	Unknown
Pension Contributions				
Annual allowance		40,000	40,000	40,000
Lifetime allowance		1.25m	1m	1m
Capital Gains Tax				
Annual exemption		11,100	11,100	Unknown
Inheritance Tax				
Nil rate band		325,000	325,000	325,000
Main residence nil rate band		n/a	n/a	100,000
Annual exemption		3,000	3,000	3,000

Notes
1. Except Scottish taxpayers: see Chapter 2.
2. Applies to interest and savings income only.
3. For married couples/civil partners if neither pays higher-rate tax
4. Higher-rate taxpayers £500, not available to additional rate taxpayers

Lightning Source UK Ltd.
Milton Keynes UK
UKOW05f2015291016
286433UK00010B/426/P